For the Record

Data Archives, Electronic Records,
Access to Information and the
Needs of the Research Community

Edited by

RENA LOHAN
MARK CONRAD
KEN HANNIGAN
JOHN A. JACKSON

INSTITUTE OF PUBLIC ADMINISTRATION

First published 1996
Institute of Public Administration
57–61 Lansdowne Road
Dublin 4
Ireland

Acknowledgements
The editors wish to express their gratitude to the Social Science Research Council, the Royal Irish Academy and the National Archives for their help and support in the publication of these proceedings.

ISBN 1 872002 63 3

British Library Cataloguing-in-Publication Data
A catalogue record for this book is available from the British Library.

Typeset in 11.5/13 Dante by Carrigboy Typesetting Services, Co. Cork
Printed by ColourBooks Ltd, Dublin

Contents

Contributors

SÉAMUS CLINCE	Principal Officer, Centre for Management and Organisation Development, Department of Finance, Dublin
MARK CONRAD	Archivist, Center for Electronic Records, National Archives and Records Administration, Washington DC
MARTIN W. DOWLING	Research Fellow, Department of Economic and Social History, Queen's University Belfast
EITHNE FITZGERALD, TD	Minister of State at the Office of the Tánaiste
ANNE GILLILAND-SWETLAND	Assistant Professor, Department of Library and Information Science, University of California, Los Angeles
KEN HANNIGAN	Senior Archivist, National Archives of Ireland
JOHN A. JACKSON	Professor of Sociology, Trinity College Dublin and Chairman, Social Science Research Council, Royal Irish Academy
LIAM KENNEDY	Reader in Economic and Social History, Queen's University Belfast
DENISE LIEVESLEY	Director, ESRC Data Archive, University of Essex

RENA LOHAN   Archivist, National Archives of
                               Ireland

MICHAEL MARSH   Senior Lecturer in Political
                               Science, Trinity College Dublin

DONAL MURPHY   Director General, Central
                               Statistics Office, Dublin

MATTI PULKKINEN   Head of Data Section, National
                               Archives of Finland

TOM QUINLAN   Archivist, National Archives of
                               Ireland

BRENDAN J. WHELAN   Head of Survey Unit, Economic
                               and Social Research Institute,
                               Dublin

Introduction

JOHN A. JACKSON

The papers collected here were presented at a one-day conference entitled 'For the Record: Data Archives, Electronic Records, Access to Information and the Needs of the Research Community', which was held in Dublin on 11 December 1995 under the auspices of the National Archives and the Social Science Research Council of the Royal Irish Academy. The National Archives was established under the National Archives Act 1986 by the formal amalgamation of the former Public Record Office of Ireland and the State Paper Office. The Act, as well as formally establishing the National Archives, introduced, in the form of a thirty-year rule, a right of public access to records of government departments and other official bodies which are listed in the schedule to the Act. The Social Science Research Council was established in 1984 following a recommendation by the Royal Irish Academy's National Committee for Economic and Social Science. Constituted on an all-Ireland basis, membership of the Council comprises a chair, three nominees from the National Committee for Economic and Social Science, and two from each of the main professional social science associations. Its principal functions are providing research grants; fostering national, cross-border and international co-operation in social science research; and encouraging the publication of research findings. Although the two bodies share little in terms of function – that of the former being primarily the preservation of government information for public use and that of the latter the promotion of research in the social sciences – their joint initiative on this occasion was the result of an increasing awareness of areas of common concern with respect to information held in electronic form.

One of the more difficult challenges facing archivists is the increasing tendency to create and store records electronically. The probable introduction of freedom of information legislation in the near future, along with the extension of existing legislation relating to data protection, will further increase the urgency with which the National Archives must establish appropriate procedures to allow it to carry out its required obligations.

In attempting to fulfil its main objective, that of supporting research in the social sciences in Ireland through the development of an appropriate infrastructure within which such research can be successfully conducted, the Social Science Research Council is committed to initiating pilot studies on data archives to ensure research access to electronic data. It was opportune, therefore, to provide, as part of this initiative, a forum to review such trends and developments; to see how they were being responded to by records creators, records managers, custodians and researchers; and to discuss a number of common concerns stemming from the increasing use of computers in the generation and storage of information.

The conference was arranged in four sessions which covered respectively:

- the current and future legislative framework for access to official information in Ireland
- the needs, concerns and expectations of the research community in Ireland in relation to official data
- case studies describing the operation of data archives and the management of electronic records in Europe
- case studies describing the operation of data archives, the management of electronic records, and research trends in the United States.[1]

A discussion which focused on the possibility of establishing a data archive in Ireland concluded the conference. The final paper published below comprises the text of a public lecture held in conjunction with the conference, under the auspices of the Faculty of Business, Economic and Social Studies, Trinity College Dublin, which set out various sources of possible support for the establishment of such an archive.

Because of continuing developments in information technology, archivists have been presented with opportunities to deliver unprecedented levels of access to archives held on traditional media, such as paper and parchment, through the creation of finding aids in electronic format. It is vital, however, that attention be focused on records created and held on computer, which may only be accessed on computer. These records are being stored on media which are notoriously unstable. Rapid changes in both hardware and software may result in such records being lost to posterity, either through physical deterioration of the storage medium, or because the technology through which this information might be accessed has become obsolete or is no longer available.

The trend towards the increasing use of technology in information management is nowhere more apparent than in public service organisations. Despite this, the rapid growth in the use of computers over the past twenty years has in practice contributed to the deterioration in the ability of central file registry systems to maintain control over the creation, movement, management and ultimate storage of records. In the long term this will result in the failure on the part of administrations to provide archival material in ordered and structured file series, which ideally should include a clear and accurate account of the movement and dissemination of information within such organisations. This deterioration of central registry filing systems will ultimately cause an actual and irretrievable loss of information in electronic form where the facilities offered to the record creator permit the uncontrolled use and unsupervised destruction of information. Apart from operational records, another vulnerable source of information stored electronically is that data, usually statistical, collected by a government agency either because of a statutory function, such as the taking of census of population, or for the purpose of formulating policy. For information managers in the public sector, control over the creation and retrieval of information has to be regained if freedom of information and data protection obligations and even business objectives are to be met. Unless steps are now taken to ensure that adequate provision is made for the preservation of such electronic records as may be considered of archival value, a comprehensive store of information may cease to be available.

For those researching in the social sciences, both in Ireland and abroad, there has been a growing body of data collected as the result of social surveys, opinion polls, specially commissioned and independent studies of specific policy areas, and analyses of official data. Thus far, however, Ireland has failed to become effectively integrated in a matrix of data centres facilitating access to and exchange of information according to agreed standards. This has meant that comparative research on a transnational basis has frequently had to exclude Ireland.

Social scientists have seen a growing sophistication of equipment to assist the analysis of data sets derived from survey data. They no longer have to grapple with the extensive manual counting and sifting of manuscript records. The arrival of mainframe computers in the early 1970s immensely increased the analytical power available to the social science researcher. As well as elaborate and complex data manipulation exercises, statistical manipulations, which had hitherto depended on subsequent use of calculators, could now be achieved as part of the process of data analysis and counting. Data handling, particularly with the development of sophisticated statistical programmes, became relatively simple and this permitted larger data sets to be introduced for analysis. The 1970s was perhaps in Irish terms the high tide of such data collection because it was still relatively cheap to collect data, while there was an increasing demand to elaborate the data collected to facilitate comparison and objectivity in analysis by ensuring a sufficient number of cases.

A data archive function is much needed in Ireland by the social science community both to collect, store and make available the data sets collected in the 1960s, 1970s and 1980s where this is still possible, and also to plan for the retention of the more modest data sets collected through the more qualitative methods in the 1990s. These very frequently take the form of tape recorded material and word processed transcripts, which again should be available in computer-readable form to other researchers. Although the sample sizes are often considerably smaller, the transcripts may be very extensive and considerable time and labour may go into their preparation.

The establishment of an Irish data archive would be one way of serving the needs of the social science research community. It would provide potential researchers with databases on which they could build their own research work, engage in comparative analysis and extend knowledge by reworking data both to test earlier findings and to apply new models. It would also encourage those undertaking research to provide deposit sets of their data for the archives so that it could be used by other researchers. The increasing cost of collecting survey data has led to a renewed interest in the use of secondary data and its analysis. This has led to a need to treat data as a cumulative resource with increasing value over time and space for comparative purposes. Although there are problems in such comparisons which arise from the unique manner in which data is collected and coded, this difficulty could be substantially overcome if attention was given to it at the outset.

This is not the first time that the question of an Irish data archive has been discussed. Earlier efforts by the social scientists to initiate a project in this regard came to nothing and the continuing absence of such a facility in Ireland has become more marked as such entities have developed in other countries and as they evolve standards to share information. Irish researchers and those wishing to research Ireland in the social sciences increasingly suffered under a disadvantage. The time is surely ripe for efforts in this regard to be made again.

While the scale of social science research activity in Ireland may not be great enough to support an independent data archive, it might be appropriate to consider the establishment of a social science data archive agency in Ireland which could act as a data registration and advisory body, and as an intermediary for the deposit of data sets in the larger European data archives. It would be able to advise researchers regarding the preparation of data for deposit and the criteria to be met, as well as helping to co-ordinate enquiries regarding the data, and acting as a publicity mechanism for the available databases throughout Europe, the United States and elsewhere. A fully functional Irish data archive, on the other hand, might also function as a place of deposit under the National Archives Act, or might function in conjunction with any future National Archives electronic archives preservation facility.

It is hoped that the publication of these papers will not only ensure continuing debate on the issues raised, but will ultimately lead to a positive resolution of the problem before much more is lost.

Notes

1 Mark Conrad, Archivist, Center for Electronic Records, National Archives and Records Administration, Washington DC, makes the following observations on the question of the differences and similarities between data archives and traditional archives which hold records in electronic form. For further treatments of these themes see the papers of Mark Conrad (pp. 64–72) and Anne Gilliland-Swetland (pp. 54–63).

> One of the themes that emerged during the course of the conference concerned the differences and similarities between data archives and traditional archives that hold electronic records. It is extremely difficult to make generalisations about the differences and similarities between the two types of organisations. Practices vary from one data archives to another and from one traditional archives to another. There are some basic similarities between the two types of organisations – both hold information in electronic form and both make that information available to researchers. In the final session of the conference, Denise Lievesley suggested that both types of organisations are concerned with preservation and access and that the primary difference between the two types of organisations is one of emphasis. She contended that data archives tend to place more emphasis on access, while traditional archives with electronic records tend to place more emphasis on preservation.
>
> One could also say that data archives tend to place greater emphasis on current research trends, while traditional archives are more concerned about long-term documentation of organisations and events. The traditional archives acquires organisational records to document the functions, policies and procedures of an organisation. The data archives develops collections of information to be preserved for (usually social science) research purposes. Data archives tend to have the products of research (i.e. survey results, census data, health statistics) making up a large portion of their collections. While traditional archives may also have products of research as part of their holdings, they will also have other organisational records, and the metadata associated with those records, so that a researcher can understand how the records were created and what they were used for. Data archives do not

normally have organisational records, other than the products of research conducted by an organisation, in their collections.

Appraisal is one function of the traditional archives that is not normally conducted by data archives. Appraisal is the process of determining what records have sufficient legal, evidential or informational value to warrant their permanent retention. In other words, do the records have continuing legal value? Do the records provide important evidence of organisational actions, policies, procedures or decisions? Do the records contain information with lasting research value – beyond the reasons for which they were originally created? These are the criteria that the traditional archives uses in selecting the records that should be permanently retained.

Data archives may concern themselves with the final criterion – do the records contain information with lasting research value? However, the data archives would probably place a greater emphasis on current researcher interest rather than lasting research value; and on information rather than records.

Freedom of Information: Building a New Culture of Openness

EITHNE FITZGERALD, TD, MINISTER OF STATE
AT THE OFFICE OF THE TÁNAISTE

The Freedom of Information Bill which comes before the Dáil shortly will mark a profound change in the way the public service relates to the public.

In drawing up the outline bill I was determined to ensure that people will be given a legal right to information held by public bodies. And public bodies – the civil service, health boards, county councils and other public agencies – will take on a legal duty to provide this information. People's legal rights to public information will be backed up by a powerful and independent appeals system.

Expanding the public's access to information

The Freedom of Information Bill will greatly expand the public's access to official information. At present, the public service operates under the Official Secrets Act, which assumes all public information is secret unless specifically authorised for public release. This Act has helped perpetuate a culture of secrecy which is out of tune with accountable and open government.

Turning the Official Secrets Act on its head

The Freedom of Information Bill will turn the culture of the Official Secrets Act on its head. It will replace the presumption of secrecy with a presumption of openness. A powerful 'purpose clause' in the bill will underline the principle that information is to be treated as freely available unless it is specifically exempt. The Freedom of Information Bill will lift the Official Secrets Act for information which is accessible under its terms.

8

The first bill ever to be published and debated in Dáil Committee in draft form, the Freedom of Information Bill has received a welcome across the party spectrum.

Making it work – a powerful appeals system

The appeals system will give the ordinary person a powerful weapon in dealing with public bodies and help ensure public confidence that the overriding principle of openness will prevail. The Ombudsman is to take on the job of Information Commissioner with the power to mediate in disputes about access to information, and to make rulings on the release of information.

The balance of the public interest

Of course there will be exemptions to the right to information. Sensitive security, defence and law enforcement information, sensitive budgetary details and negotiation strategy will remain protected. The rights of individuals to privacy will be respected. But ultimately in deciding whether information in exempt categories can be made available, the overriding test will be whether the balance of the public interest lies in disclosure or in withholding the information concerned.

Going far beyond access through the courts

At present, in exceptional circumstances, people can access official documents through the discovery process in the courts. The *Ambiorix* case established that the right of discovery can extend even to Cabinet papers, where the applicant can show he or she has a legal interest and the documents are relevant. Enacting a Freedom of Information Bill will not change anyone's right to go to court and seek documents in these circumstances. The right to official information will not however be confined to those with the money to go to the High Court, and those who can show they have a legal interest in particular documents. Access to information will be open to everyone. It will be simple, accessible and cheap. Anyone will be able to look for information over the counter, and to get information for the cost of photocopying. If the volume of information sought is large, additional charges may arise where there is significant search time involved.

To help people find what they are looking for, each public body will publish a manual or guide to what it does and what kind of information it keeps. These will be available in public libraries and offices throughout the country. Public servants will have a legal duty to help people to pinpoint the information they are looking for. On the other side, people looking for information will also be expected, under the bill, to be reasonably precise. Getting these details right is important, because a harassed public service may be less enthusiastic about the value of openness. I want to build a system which is simple and user-friendly.

Openness – a key democratic value

Open government goes to the heart of a democratic society. Information is power. Freedom of information is about sharing that power, about making administration responsive to the needs of individual citizens, making government more accountable to the people it serves, and opening up new possibilities for democratic participation.

Freedom of information will deliver a permanent shift in the balance of power between the citizen and the state. Access to information will be a right, not a privilege.

Owning the information which governs our lives

I want to see people owning the information which governs their lives. People will be able to access, and correct if necessary, any files held on them by government departments and other public agencies. They will be able to see the rules, regulations and internal guidelines by which their dealings with the state are assessed. And people will be entitled to see the full reasons underlying any administrative decisions which affect them.

People's dealings with public bodies are wide-ranging and important, covering areas like tax, education, health, housing, business and farming grants, and child benefits. Over a million adults depend on the state for their incomes through the social welfare system. Freedom of information will be a powerful tool in giving a right to access information about decisions that are central to people's lives. It will help guarantee careful, accurate, fair and professional record keeping about individual citizens, and will be a powerful protection against arbitrary decision making.

Accountability and improved decision making

All jurisdictions with freedom of information legislation have seen a clear improvement in the quality of public service administration. Openness is the best guarantee the citizen can have in the quality of public service.

Drawing on best international practice

The Irish Freedom of Information Bill follows in the steps of other democracies: Sweden, which enacted such legislation in 1766; Finland in 1951; the USA in 1966; Norway and Denmark in 1970; France and the Netherlands in 1978; and Australia, Canada and New Zealand in 1982.

In coming late in the day to freedom of information legislation, we have been in a unique position to draw on best international practice in framing our own legislation. Our legislative proposals have been particularly influenced by the experience of freedom of information in the common law countries of Australia, Canada and New Zealand, each based like ourselves on a Westminster model of government.

New insights into public policy

The enactment of the National Archives Act has given historians and students great insights into Irish public policy, up to the last thirty years. Freedom of information will bring a new era of openness to contemporary decision making. While protecting documents relating to decisions which have not yet been reached, the underlying principle in the Freedom of Information Bill is that after a decision is taken, relevant papers can be released.

This potential to look back at how decisions were reached has proved in other countries to be an important factor in improving the quality of analysis and advice underlying public decision making. Everywhere we studied, we were told how the standard of the public service improved on enactment of freedom of information legislation.

The National Archives, Electronic Records and Freedom of Information

KEN HANNIGAN

The National Archives of Ireland has existed under this name only since 1988 when the National Archives Act 1986 came into effect, although the constituent parts of the organisation which was created by that Act, the State Paper Office and the Public Record Office of Ireland, had existed separately for long before and had been part of a de facto amalgamation since the late nineteenth century.

The Public Record Office was formally established under an Act of 1867 and housed in a purpose-built repository at the Four Courts in Dublin. The legislation which established it also declared that records of the courts and certain other official records must be preserved and transferred to the Public Record Office after certain prescribed periods.

The State Paper Office, which had existed since 1702 and was housed in the Record Tower in Dublin Castle from the beginning of the nineteenth century, contained the records of the Chief Secretary's Office and its constituent departments, comprising the records of central government administration in Ireland. Following the establishment of the Public Record Office in 1867, records older than fifty years were due to be transferred to it from the State Paper Office on an incremental basis. In fact by 1922 records as far back as 1790 remained in the State Paper Office and so escaped the appalling destruction which occurred when the Public Record Office was burned to the ground that year at the beginning of the Civil War. The surviving State Paper Office collections continued to be housed in the Record Tower of Dublin Castle until the early 1990s. The reading room there was closed in 1990 and the rest of the building was vacated in 1991 following the allocation of premises in Bishop Street in Dublin to the National Archives.

Although the Public Record Office was reconstituted following the destruction of 1922, it remained for the next fifty years, the first fifty years of the independent Irish state, a demoralised and weakened institution. It continued to operate under the legislation of 1867 and the parochial records Acts of 1875 and 1876, but had no statutory responsibility for the bulk of records created by government departments and agencies.

From the early 1970s, however, there was a growing demand, mostly from historians, for access to official archival information and for legislation governing the disposition of official documentation. This culminated in the introduction of the National Archives Act which became law in 1986 and was brought into operation in June 1988. As well as liberalising access to official records, and other provisions described below, the Act formally amalgamated the Public Record Office and the State Paper Office. It also allowed for what was in effect a two and a half year period following its coming into operation in which departmental records older than thirty years were to be transferred to the newly created National Archives unless certified for retention or disposal. Within this two and a half year period, therefore, the accumulated backlog of departmental records going back to the foundation of the state and beyond had to be transferred to the National Archives and made available for public inspection. The formal amalgamation of the Public Record Office and the State Paper Office, the anticipated deluge of departmental records, and the actual and anticipated increase in the number of readers using the National Archives, necessitated a move into new premises. The building in Bishop Street, on the site of the former Jacobs' biscuit factory, had been reconstructed as a paper store for the Government Supplies Agency. The main attraction of the site for the National Archives is the potential it holds for the construction of a purpose-built repository which would cater for accommodation needs into the new century. As of now this potential remains to be realised. The building became the new headquarters of the National Archives in 1992 and, with the opening of the new reading room there at the beginning of that year, the former reading room in the Four Courts closed to the public.

The number of people using the National Archives has been growing remarkably since the early 1970s. There were 19,422 visits to the National Archives by members of the public in 1995 – a higher number than ever before. In fact the number of readers visiting the National Archives has shown a tenfold increase since the early 1970s and shows every sign of continuing to increase, reflecting an increasing demand for access to official information. Yet we still only have about the same number of staff as we had in the mid-1970s, and indeed for much of the 1980s our staff resources remained at a lower level than in the 1970s. The massive increase in the number of people using the National Archives means, therefore, that most of our resources are occupied in providing a service to the public on a daily basis – as opposed, say, to developing strategies for the management of electronic records or developing a centre for electronic records.

While the numbers using the National Archives have increased dramatically in this period, our responsibilities have also been transformed. The National Archives Act gives us considerable powers in relation to official records. The main points of the Act can be summarised as follows:

1. All departmental records must be preserved, unless their destruction is authorised in writing by the National Archives.

2. In general all departmental records which are more than thirty years old must be transferred to the National Archives and made available for inspection by the public. Particular records may be retained by departments only if they are covered by certificates stating either:

   (i) that they are in regular use in a department or are required in connection with its administration, or

   (ii) that they should not be made available for public inspection on one of the grounds specified in the Act, the grounds being that to make them available:

   (a) would be contrary to the public interest

   (b) would or might constitute a breach of statutory duty, or a breach of good faith on the ground that they contained information supplied in confidence, or

   (c) would or might cause distress or danger to living persons on the ground that they contain information about individuals, or would be likely to lead to an action for damages or defamation.

Since the National Archives Act came into force, most government departments have processed their records which are older than thirty years for transfer or retention.

While almost all government departments and a number of major government offices have transferred most of their records, much of the wider public service has yet to transfer records. There is still, therefore, a vast quantity of paper-based records yet to be processed.

If a department or agency wishes to dispose of records, it must apply to the National Archives for authorisation. Staff of the National Archives carry out an appraisal of the files in question, and the Director of the National Archives, if satisfied on the basis of the appraisal report that the records do not warrant preservation, signs a certificate authorising their disposal. The process is documented at each stage. Sometimes authorisation to dispose is conditional on a representative sample of the records being preserved. A condition of the authorisation might be, for instance, that one file in every hundred be preserved.

When files are being withheld under Section 8(4) of the Act, the certificate withholding the records must be signed both by an officer within the department who has been specifically designated as a Certifying Officer, and by an officer in the Department of the Taoiseach who has been designated as a Consenting Officer. There is provision for withholding part of a file rather than the entire file, if it is felt that the rest of the file can be released to public inspection. This is something which to date has been infrequently used. For traditional paper records it can be a cumbersome process and one which is difficult to administer. For large series of structured electronic records, however, where it is possible, for instance, to withhold the fields containing sensitive information such as personal identifiers, the partial release of such records at an earlier stage in their lives will become easier to administer.

In general the National Archives will not take possession of records which are closed to the public. Such records generally remain in the custody of the creating agency and must be preserved by that agency until such time as the records are transferred to the National Archives for public inspection or until their disposal is authorised.

The National Archives Act is media transparent. All departmental records are covered by it, regardless of whether they are files in the traditional sense or computer records. In fact Section 2(2) of the Act specifically includes magnetic tapes, magnetic disks, optical or video disks and other machine-readable records within the definition of the term 'Departmental Records'.

As yet we have not had to deal with a request to accept the transfer of computerised records to the National Archives, nor have we had an application for the disposal of any such records. Given that computers only began to be used in any general way in the civil service during the 1970s and were then confined to large batch processing operations on mainframes, one might expect to wait until the new millennium until anything other than paper records would be due for transfer to the National Archives, and it would probably be well into the next century before the National Archives would be receiving any electronic records other than data sets. If we wait another ten or fifteen years before acting, however, we will be in serious trouble. In terms of maintaining access to these records we may already be in trouble.

There are two aspects to this that cause concern. First, it is hardly conceivable that departments are keeping all their electronic records, especially as another Act, the Data Protection Act, actually encourages disposal, and yet we have not had a single request for authorisation to dispose of them. Second, whether or not departments are actively disposing of their computerised records, unless they are taking steps to actively *preserve* them the end result will be the same. In most cases a positive effort is required to dispose of traditional paper documents. Unless the conditions are very unfavourable indeed, records stored in basements and cellars survive. With electronic records the opposite is the case; it requires a conscious decision to preserve them, to migrate them onwards. In fact it requires a continuing and, it would seem, never-ending series of conscious decisions.

In this context it is important to remember what Section 7(1) of the National Archives Act states:

> Departmental records shall, unless they are transferred to the National Archives in accordance with section 8 or disposed of under subsection (5), be retained and preserved in the Department of State in which they were made or are held.

Does this refer to all records? Yes. Even to e-mail? Yes. This is the law as it stands at the moment. It places a major responsibility on government departments and on the National Archives to ensure that archival electronic records are properly catered for.

For archives there are many problems posed by electronic records but they can be arranged under two broad headings in the areas of preservation and records management.

Firstly there are the archival problems relating to preservation and access. There is as yet no proven long-term storage medium for electronic records, as electronic records. Magnetic tape, which seems to be the preferred long-term storage medium of most electronic records centres and data archives, is notoriously unstable, whereas optical disks seem to be universally distrusted. At least with paper we can tell at a glance if the record is still legible. With tape it must be mounted and read electronically; it must be periodically rewound and retensioned. To be safe, several copies must be made and stored in different locations.

On the other hand, electronic records *can* be copied easily. It is no longer necessary, therefore, to have all your eggs in one basket – you can have the same egg in several baskets at once. With the densities being achieved on storage media at the moment, it is possible to store vast quantities of data in very small spaces. For a traditional archivist, the most surprising feature of electronic records centres and data archives is how little physical space they need to store their records. The centre for electronic records in the US National Archives has almost double the staff of the entire National Archives of Ireland and has no difficulty in demonstrating that in terms of the job it has to do it is under-resourced. Yet its entire holdings fit in a section of one room. It is with a sense of wonder and of joy that a traditional archivist, constantly labouring with problems of space, sees the entire holdings of the ESRC Data Archives represented on a shelf of DAT tape. There are possibilities here for archives undreamt of a generation ago.

One of the great ironies of the situation becomes apparent: it is possible to preserve everything; it is easier to lose everything. There are two factors which pose potentially greater threats than media instability and these are hardware and software obsolescence. We have all experienced the bewildering speed of change in this area. Even if a medium were devised on which with some confidence electronic records could be permanently stored, there would still be no guarantee that in twenty or even ten years' time it would be possible to find a functioning machine still capable of reading the medium or a software program still capable of interpreting the data stored on it. Even with more stable storage media, therefore, it will be necessary to migrate data from machines which are obsolescent to machines which will promise functionality for another brief period, to migrate data from software programs as they are updated, or to ensure backward compatibility. It will also be necessary to preserve the metadata containing all the information about how the data were created and stored, and about the software program which created them.

Were we to proceed in the traditional way of archivists, coming to appraise these records when they cease to be current or when they are released into the public domain in thirty years' or even twenty years' time, it may be impossible to access or appraise them. It is more than likely that this situation has already been reached with some records. We have heard of archival institutions abroad being pressed to take possession of thousands of reels of magnetic tape with no documentation, no record of what machines or what programs created them, no very clear idea of what was on them.

The second area of concern relates to what has been called the distributed environment in which electronic records are being created, brought about by the breakdown of central registries and filing systems. The years which in Ireland have seen a greater public awareness of the value of archives and the introduction of legislation in this area have also been the years in which there has been a breakdown in the traditional record-keeping systems which were often the best guarantors of the survival of these records.

Public servants now tend to be more autonomous in managing their own information but also tend to be more possessive of it. Individuals type their own documents and file them on the hard drives of their PCs. If they are stored on networked systems they are frequently held in personal directories, guarded by passwords or filed in a haphazard way. The proliferation of personal computers has been accompanied by a trend towards decentralisation. With the disappearance of central file registries from government departments, the corporate memory has been dissipated. Across the civil service one finds a multiplicity of systems, a multiplicity of software packages being used on them, a multiplicity of drafts and duplicates being stored in them. Ken Thibodeau, who heads the Center for Electronic Records in the United States National Archives, states that in his experience US government agencies have versions of just about every software package over a range of applications and have also invented a few of their own, and there is no reason to think that the situation in Ireland is any different.

Computers make it infinitely easier to manage vast quantities of information, to search vast data banks for specific items, to create indexes at the touch of a few keys, but at the same time permit, almost guarantee, the creation of such vast quantities of drafts, duplicates and trivia as to make the task of identifying the historically significant almost impossible. How does one begin to appraise the accumulated e-mail of a large organisation built up over a period of years?

We know that we must act now to ensure that the records which have to date been created electronically and are at this moment being created electronically will be accessible in the future. It is clear that the decision to preserve must be made earlier in the life-cycle of an electronic record than has been the case with paper records. Until now, decisions about the long-term preservation of records were generally made at the end of the active life of the record. This decision must now be brought forward to the beginning of the life-cycle. It may be brought forward even further so that one might say even before records are created that all records of a certain type will be preserved and others will be authorised for routine disposal or deletion. Written into the programs in which such records are created will be the mechanism for ensuring their continued preservation. Such records will be tagged at birth.

There are converging interests here which make it important, not just for the National Archives or for future historians, that information is properly managed now. If the corporate memory of a government department or agency breaks down this is not just a problem for the archives or for future researchers. Agencies will be more accountable for their records under the proposed Freedom of Information Act and the extension of data protection, and it is clearly in the interests of the civil service generally that information is efficiently used. There is no conflict here with archival considerations but rather a convergence of different priorities.

All this is acknowledged. Other agencies within the civil service are also concerned about the loss of control over information. The Department of Finance has commenced work on developing a model for the more efficient management of information in the civil service (see below Séamus Clince, pp. 27–34). Section 19(3) of the National Archives Act empowers the Minister for Finance to make regulations in consultation with the Director of the National Archives for the proper management and preservation of departmental records in the custody or care of a department of state and there is clearly a need here for regulations governing the proper management of electronic records.

There are a number of options for the preservation of archival electronic records in the longer term. First, the National Archives may proceed as at present and assume that electronic records will be preserved by the creating agencies until such time as they are due for transfer to the National Archives. This is, after all, all that is required under the law as it now stands. In a few years' time we may be faced with having to deal with the records generated by the early large mainframes. At that point we might try to acquire the technical resources necessary to preserve these records and make them available. A few years further on we would have to begin dealing with the records created by PCs and PC networks. Even making the most optimistic assumptions – that the records would survive and would be accessible at that stage – being compelled to deal with such records thirty years after their creation would put us at an enormous disadvantage. Much of the time would be spent in trying to grasp or re-create the concepts and technologies of an earlier age. This scenario appears ridiculous and yet with every year that passes it becomes more likely. If things proceed along these lines, the next generation of archivists will find that their predecessors, then enjoying retirement, have left them with a huge gap in the records.

Second, an electronic records centre might be established as part of the National Archives and we would begin as soon as possible to accession records into it. If we are going to have to deal with these records in the future, we can avoid many of the problems we would have to face then by confronting them now. This has already been done in some National Archives, such as those in the United States, Canada, France and Sweden. In the best of all possible worlds this might be the best solution. But there are arguments against this strategy also. The resources required to run an electronic records centre in which the archival electronic records of the entire civil service would be centralised would be considerable and would require a degree of specialisation which we do not at present have. The ESRC Data Archive now employs more than forty staff, and this is presumably the minimum required to run a large data archive. On the computing and data processing side alone there are nine staff at Essex, including programmers, machine operators and data processors. At the moment in the National Archives we do not have a single IT specialist. Even if we were suddenly given all the resources required to run an electronic records centre, there would still be a major question as to whether centralisation of electronic records in what would still be primarily a traditional archives would necessarily be the best thing for electronic records. There is a great debate raging within the archival profession in the United States on this score. It has been said that, in the electronic age, custody of archives which may require the ongoing maintenance of a range of hardware and software and continuing migration of both data and applications will put records in archival custody at relatively greater risk than those which remain in the physical custody of the agencies that created them.[1]

This leads to a third option. There is certainly a very strong case to be made for the creating agencies to retain physical control of their electronic records and to be responsible for their continued preservation, and ultimately for their accessibility. This seems to be what is happening in Australia. In an electronic age physical custody of the records per se becomes less important and location in every sense immaterial. It may be just as easy to access electronic records remotely as at a central location. Remote access to catalogues is already the reality with some archives, and particularly libraries, and there is no reason why remote access to electronic records themselves should not soon be the norm. Freedom of information legislation will force official agencies to grant access to records during their active life and this will mean in turn that agencies will have to ensure that points of access and adequate finding aids are provided for such records. Freedom of information legislation will also regulate the creation and management of official records within these agencies. It would be the responsibility of the creating agencies to migrate data, to ensure that when new technology is being acquired, data are transported safely from the old system to the new. This is considerably more feasible if done within the creating institution than if done by someone unfamiliar with the original software application or the computer system on which the information was previously created or stored. The role of the National Archives in this scenario might be to maintain intellectual rather than physical control over such records, perhaps to operate a central information locator system for archival electronic records. The reverse side of the case for indefinite retention by the creating agencies is that although the law might require that departments and agencies maintain their records over time, preservation of non-current records would not otherwise be high on the priorities of most organisations. Ensuring access to live information through a Freedom of Information Act may be one thing; convincing agencies that they must not only preserve such information, but must also preserve the means of ensuring access to it over time, perhaps for ever, is another thing entirely. Archives are in the business of everlasting life; most other organisations are not. The organisations themselves will come and go. As things stand, when departments are broken up or amalgamated the question of who keeps what files can be a difficult one. Even if it were decided that the National Archives should pursue a non-custodial policy in relation to electronic records, we would soon be faced with the problem of catering for the records of entities such as tribunals or commissions of enquiry which are of short duration.

A fourth option would be for the purely physical task of preserving electronic records to be contracted out to a commercial

concern. There are a number of data warehouses already in existence which store and retrieve electronic records on a commercial
basis. There are many fairly obvious reasons why this would be an
unlikely solution for government. Cost and security are two.

Finally, there is the possibility of using an already existing facility
such as a specialised data archives or library. The big problem here
of course is that there is no such entity at present existing in Ireland.
If there were, it would at least in theory be feasible for that organisation either to become a place of deposit under the National
Archives Act for the long-term preservation of electronic records
(part of the National Archives for the purpose of the Act) or to act
as a repository for the medium-term preservation of electronic
records which might ultimately find a permanent home in the
National Archives. Again there is something of a convergence of
interest here. The need for such a facility is currently being stressed
by some within the social science community in Europe, not as a
long-term repository of historical information, but to encourage
uniform standards in the area of information gathering and
exchange. Preservation of historical records over large time-frames
might not be the primary business of a data archives. Many such
entities keep records for their current research value rather than
for their historical or evidential value – 'use it or lose it' is a maxim
sometimes used in relation to data held by data libraries. However,
there is much common ground and much potential common
ground here and surely there is no very strong argument against a
data archives also functioning as a historical archives. In a country
as small as Ireland it surely makes sense to pool available resources.
In Denmark, a previously existing data archives which developed
in an academic context has been absorbed into the state archives
system, and in England and Wales it seems that the Public Record
Office has decided that the preservation of electronic records will
be outsourced to an existing data archives. While an Irish data
archives might not actually become a place of deposit under the
National Archives Act, or function as a medium-term repository for
official electronic records, at the very least the existence of a data
archives might ensure the preservation in the short term of some
data sets which might otherwise be lost, allowing us the luxury of
time to decide what should happen in the long term. In the event of

a centre for electronic records being established within the National Archives, the prior existence of a data archives might also ensure that there would be on hand a pool of expertise from which we might draw.

It is likely that the solution will be found not through one of these options but through a combination of them.

In conclusion, though the long-term preservation of electronic records is a source of worry for archivists the world over, it should also be remembered that electronic records present us with great opportunities. Some of these have been mentioned already:

- it is possible to store so much data in so little space
- it is possible to copy records with great ease and rapidity and therefore ensure there is at least one security copy of every record stored separately from the original
- it is possible to transfer copies of electronic records into archival custody early in the life-cycle of the records, and even where the records are sensitive, to make public use or anonymised versions of the records available at an early stage
- it becomes possible to provide simultaneous access to the same records for countless numbers of researchers and it will no longer be necessary for them to physically visit the archives in order to access the records. It becomes possible to provide a degree of public access to archives undreamt of until very recently. We have in the last year, through the operation of our own World Wide Web pages on the Internet, become aware of some of these possibilities.

Though there are major causes for concern in the short to medium term concerning the current generation of electronic records, and these require urgent action, in the longer term there is every reason to hope the difficulties encountered by archives in dealing with the records generated by the new technologies will themselves be solved by reference to the new technologies.

Notes

1 For a discussion of these arguments see especially David Bearman
   and Margaret Hedstrom, 'Reinventing Archives for Electronic
   Records: Alternative Service Delivery Options', in *Electronic Records
   Management Program Strategies (Archives and Museum Informatics
   Technical Report No. 18)*, Pittsburgh, 1993.

A Framework for Information Management in the Irish Civil Service

SÉAMUS CLINCE

In this paper I will provide a broad overview of IT in the civil service as a backdrop to a discussion of the information management issues facing the civil service and a framework to help resolve those issues.

Overview of IT in the civil service

The civil service has a staff of 27,000 and we currently spend approximately £45 million per annum on IT, not including IT staff costs. This investment has grown considerably over the past ten years so that, while there are a number of large mainframe-type installations, the technical environment is predominantly based on a modern client/server architecture. The uses of IT are as varied as the departments which make up the civil service. So, the investment is large, the infrastructure is modern and the use is diverse.

Responsibility for IT rests with individual departments, while central co-ordination and support are provided by the Centre for Management and Organisation Development (CMOD) in the Department of Finance.

What are the major IT issues? At this stage we do not see technology itself as an issue – the major technical challenge is the ability to mix and combine available and emerging technologies to meet business needs. The major issues are in the non-technical area:

- how to achieve maximum benefits from IT
- how to use IT as a facilitator of beneficial organisation development, and

- how to use IT to address the wide range of information management issues facing the civil service as we career towards the end of the century.

Information management issues

The civil service is facing an unprecedented number of challenges and opportunities in the area of information management. Many of them are common to all large organisations while some are specific to our environment. Let me briefly mention the major ones.

The Strategic Management Initiative and public service reform

The Strategic Management Initiative (SMI) is, among other things, asking each department and office to clarify and implement its objectives at organisation, process and performer levels. It is already clear that improved information systems are essential to support the more results- and performance-oriented civil service emerging from the SMI.

The government is expected to announce shortly a significant public sector reform programme arising largely from the SMI. This will add further to the demand for improved information systems, particularly in areas such as financial and personnel management.

'Information age' demands

The Irish civil service must follow the example being set by other countries such as the USA and Denmark by providing client-focused services, for example 'one-stop service centres', electronic publishing and electronic commerce. If the goals of the information society in terms of universal access to information networks are to be met, new information access demands will arise over time. For example, clients may want to submit service requests electronically and subsequently monitor their progress through the work process.

Freedom of information

The proposed Freedom of Information Bill will have significant implications for information systems in departments as pressure grows to provide easy access to a wide range of information, much of it currently held in what might be politely described as an unstructured way.

National archives

The demands arising from national archiving requirements also create a need for a more organised way of storing and processing information and documents. One of the major challenges will be to combine information from paper-based and electronic files.

Justification of IT investments

The level of investment in IT continues to rise and new forms of justification are required as the emphasis shifts from the traditional project-based investments to enterprise-level investments and incremental benefits. The implications of this for information management are that comprehensive information management requires this enterprise-wide investment and we must seek information-related benefits as part of the justification argument.

Need for a comprehensive framework

If all relevant information in an organisation is to be managed in an integrated way, as it must be to address some of these issues, methods must be found to embrace all the existing sources of information (paper files, traditional transaction processing systems, office systems, etc.) within a coherent framework.

Loss of discipline

When I commenced my civil service career there was a strong discipline in the way information was recorded on official files and in the way those files were managed. Such discipline no longer pertains, even for paper files in some cases, and certainly not in the world of word processing and electronic mail. While I do not suggest that we should return to the extreme rigour of earlier days, we must find an appropriate balance and, fortunately, modern software allows us to do so.

Responding to the challenge

Even one of these issues is enough to cause sleepless nights for the conscientious IT or information manager; the combination of issues may turn the sleepless nights into a nightmare. However, just as necessity is the mother of invention, nightmares can spawn dreams. We believe that the civil service requires a comprehensive information management policy to respond to these issues and we have commenced work on development of such a policy, which would include:

- co-ordinated information collection from the public, business and specialised information bases, perhaps along the lines planned in Denmark, where it is proposed that ministries should not be permitted to seek information which has already been supplied to another ministry
- sophisticated IT-based systems to store, process and disseminate information in a co-ordinated, yet flexible client-focused, way (including use of the Internet, public access kiosks and, in due course, interactive TV)
- legislation and procedures to address the many legal issues involved in full electronic working
- a framework for the coherent management of the diverse information sources within a department.

Because of its relevance to this conference, I will deal for the rest of this paper with the final element.

Proposed Information Management Reference Model

We consider that the first step in moving towards a coherent framework for information management is agreement on an Information Management Reference Model to which future IT developments in the civil service should conform. The model is illustrated in Figure 1. It contains four elements which interact with each other:

- work support systems (including, where appropriate, process management facilities)

- a central filing system
- management information systems
- a standards-based long-term archive.

Figure 1: Information Management Reference Model

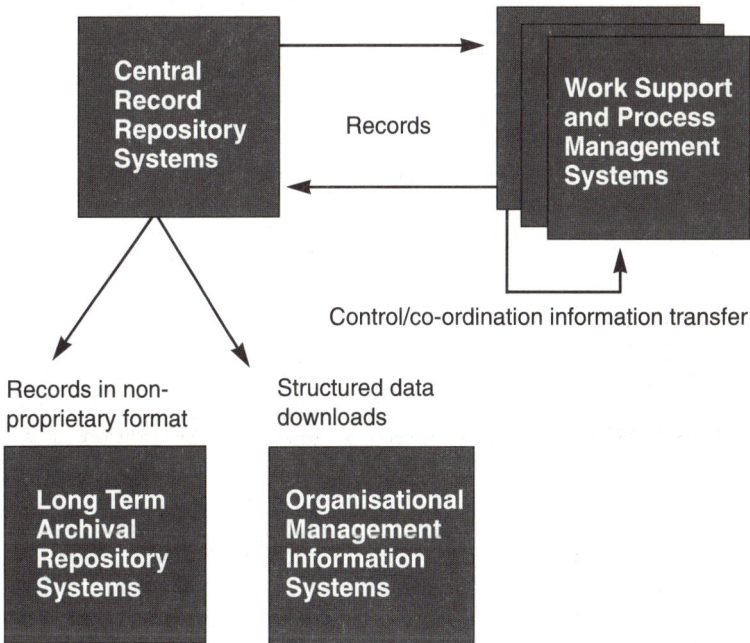

Work Support and Process Management Systems (WSPMS)

A WSPMS is a comprehensive system catering in an integrated way for all of the information needed for the process concerned – structured data and unstructured information (letters, forms, faxes, electronic mail, documents, minutes, etc.). Each WSPMS would be designed to facilitate the specific needs of a work group, and would give members of that group access to the IT facilities and information needed. A WSPMS could also provide process management facilities such as:

- electronically routing information and work commitments between team members

- rules to determine that a task is done completely
- showing the status of work-in-progress, cycle and waiting times, etc.
- facilitating results/performance-oriented analysis.

Central Record Repository and Record Retrieval Systems (CRR)

The CRR stores information transferred from the WSPMSs. This is required to:

- manage long-term storage requirements
- allow the stored information from a number of WSPMSs to be searched in different ways
- provide a range of facilities necessary for organisation-wide information management (registration, version control, etc.).

Organisational Management Information Systems

These systems would support reporting and analysis requirements not met by the facilities in the WSPMSs or the CRR. For example, they could:

- monitor resource usage (e.g. staff involved in application processing)
- analyse statistics (e.g. ratio of outstanding claims to completed claims)
- identify trends (e.g. increases in requests, or changes in request types from specific clients)
- monitor critical business 'alerts' (e.g. SMI targets being missed).

Relevant data would be transferred to this system from the CRR. Data transfer could be immediate, daily, weekly or monthly as appropriate.

The data in these systems would be stored in formats supported by popular analysis tools such as

- SQL-based relational files
- multidimensional file systems for access by on-line analytical processing tools (OLAP).

Long-Term Archival System

The source of the information in this system is the CRR: information with an archive flag set would be transferred from the CRR when it reached archiving age. All of the information held in this system would be unalterable.

This archival repository would comply with the, as yet unknown, access requirements of the National Archives, and all transferred information would be in standards-based formats. When these access needs are known, they will determine the amount of data which must be transferred from the CRR, together with the searching and structuring capabilities to be provided by the archives access software.

Interaction between the elements

The proposed framework implies considerable interaction between the four elements. For example:

- all work support systems must be able to transfer information to the central information system
- the central information system must be capable of transferring information to the long-term standards-based archives and also to the management information systems.

Within a department/office, each of these interactions would be standardised and common across the whole organisation. Improved discipline would be achieved because the interactions would largely be automatic. Ideally, subsets of these standards would be common across all organisations in the civil service to allow, for example, organisations to be aggregated or disaggregated, or information and work commitments to be transferred between organisations.

Implementation of the model

The elements within the reference model are highly modular. Organisations can, therefore, take on the full consequences of the model in phases. For example, an organisation with no investment in work support systems could begin to build such systems one at a time, taking the interaction requirements into account, and at later stages could commission the other elements. Alternatively, an organisation with some existing investment in work support systems could retrofit them with functionality needed to support the interaction requirement and work onwards from there.

Conclusion

We are not suggesting that this will be easy or that it can be achieved in the short term. However, the issues and challenges cannot be ignored and we believe that the time is right to start responding to them.

The Role of the Central Statistics Office in Facilitating Research

DONAL MURPHY

Introduction

The Central Statistics Office (CSO) collects a wide range of economic and social data which has considerable potential for research purposes. Because of pressure of work demands, CSO priority is necessarily given to the publication of analyses for general users. CSO staff have over the years regularly published more detailed analyses and special analyses are also provided on request. There is considerable further potential to be exploited, and the CSO facilitates bona fide researchers.

Researchers and research bodies are generally assisted free of charge subject, of course, to the constraints of the statutory provisions under which the CSO operates and resource implications. A fee is charged, however, for special analyses provided to commercial bodies and to researchers involved in paid consultancy work.

Constraints

The principal constraint in allowing researchers direct access to CSO microdata bases is the statutory obligation to preserve the identity of the data suppliers. The confidentiality of data provided by survey respondents was guaranteed by the Statistics Act 1926 and further reinforced by the Statistics Act 1993 which came into operation in November 1994.

Survey respondents are explicitly told that the data they provide will be treated as strictly confidential and the CSO goes to extreme lengths to ensure this. It has a long-standing reputation in this regard. Any breaches, even inadvertently, would undermine the confidence of survey respondents in the Office and adversely affect their response. The CSO is not prepared to take any risks in this regard.

Facilities available to researchers

The Statistics Act 1926 imposed very stringent confidentiality constraints to the extent of precluding outside access to any data relating to individual survey respondents even if such data could not be directly or indirectly related to them. The CSO sought the opinion of the Attorney General on this latter interpretation a number of times; it was confirmed on each occasion. Under these restrictive provisions the only manner by which the CSO could facilitate researchers was:

1. provision of custom designed analyses
2. application of computer programs written by researchers to CSO microdata bases
3. allowing researchers direct access to data within the CSO as Officers of Statistics appointed under the provisions of the Statistics Act.

In drafting the Statistics Act 1993 the opportunity was taken to incorporate other provisions to facilitate researchers. These included:

4. provision of anonymised microdata sets
5. undertaking surveys jointly with other public authorities and persons
6. access to census of population returns after 100 years.

Provision of custom designed analyses

The CSO generally publishes only a small proportion of the possible analyses for any survey. However, it provides custom designed analyses on request to meet particular needs. Many researchers are facilitated in this manner.

Application of researchers' programs to CSO microdata bases

On occasions the analyses required by researchers involve extensive programming and exploratory analyses which the CSO would not be able to undertake because of the resource implications. In these circumstances the CSO is prepared to give the data base specifications to researchers, run computer programs written by them on the data, and return the printouts after verifying that confidential data is not being inadvertently divulged. This approach requires the researcher to have specialist IT skills. It has been availed of only by the Economic and Social Research Institute (in the case of the Household Budget Survey).

Direct access as Officers of Statistics

The Statistics Act allows non-CSO persons to be appointed Officers of Statistics to work on data collected under the Act. This is a formal process and the persons appointed are subject to the data protection and other (e.g. penalties) provisions of the Act. In practice, they are allowed access to data only within the CSO and are not permitted to take any identifiable data off the premises. This facility also permits the CSO to engage outside consultants or indeed academic staff who may wish to spend sabbatical leave working in the CSO.

Provision of anonymised microdata sets

This facility is now permitted under the Statistics Act 1993. It allows the CSO to provide anonymised microdata sets to a particular research body or researcher under conditions and restrictions determined by the Director General. Such data sets will be provided under a formal agreement with the particular researcher which will impose strict confidentiality conditions. The arrangement will only operate for personal and household data as microdata relating to businesses cannot be adequately anonymised.

Joint surveys

The 1993 Act allows the CSO to undertake surveys jointly with other public authorities or persons, with both parties having access to the data collected. The critical feature here is that survey respondents will knowingly participate under this data-sharing arrangement.

Access to census returns after 100 years

The Statistics Act 1926 precluded public access to returns made to censuses of population since the foundation of the state. Because of their historical and genealogical value these records have been preserved by the CSO and special provision was made in the 1993 Act to allow public access to them after 100 years – i.e. the 1926 census records can be made available as public records in 2026.

At present the returns for three censuses (1926, 1936 and 1946) are held by the National Archives and the CSO has requested the National Archives to take custody of the returns for subsequent censuses to ensure that they are stored in appropriate archival conditions. The returns for the 1901 and 1911 censuses have been public records since 1961 and are available for public inspection in the National Archives. This was possible because the legislation under which they were taken did not make any specific reference to the confidentiality of the returns. They were transferred to the Public Record Office (integrated as part of the National Archives when it was established in 1988) by the Minister for Justice by means of a warrant made under the Public Records (Ireland) Act 1867. The primary motivation was to make them freely available to solicitors for legal purposes. However, they have become the most frequently accessed records in the National Archives for genealogical, historical and other purposes.

The records for earlier censuses are not available because:

- returns for the 1813, 1821, 1831–4, 1841 and 1851 censuses were destroyed when the record repository of the Public Record Office was burnt down in 1922 (some returns survive for seven of the thirty-two counties)
- returns for the 1861 and 1871 censuses were deliberately destroyed shortly after the censuses were taken
- returns for the 1881 and 1891 censuses were pulped for paper because of the paper shortage during the First World War.

Consequently the returns for the 1901 census are the earliest now surviving intact.

Other CSO services available

Other CSO services of use to researchers include:

1. *Library:* This is the most extensively stocked statistical library in the country. In addition to national publications it contains the statistical publications of international organisations (e.g. Eurostat, OECD, ILO, UN) and many countries. The main library is located in the Cork office (Skehard Road) but the main publications are also available in a smaller library in Dublin (Ardee Road, Rathmines).

2. *Data Bank (EireStat):* This contains about 8,700 time series and 4,000 cross-sectional variables. It is not generally accessible on-line at present. A monthly diskette service is provided.

3. *Census Inquiry Service:* A vast quantity of information is available from the various censuses of population. A dedicated service is available to facilitate user requests for particular categories of information. A standard set of small area population statistics (SAPS) is also available for urban districts, rural districts, towns, district electoral divisions, etc.

4. *Foreign Trade Inquiry Service:* As the full range of detail available on foreign trade statistics cannot be published a service is available to provide users with details at the level of tariff by country and Standard International Trade Classification (SITC) by country on magnetic tape, microfiche or computer printout.

5. *Guide to CSO Publications and Information Services:* This annual guide is available free of charge from the Information Section (Cork).

Finally, it is essential that researchers and other users of CSO statistics are fully conversant with the methodology used. The Office welcomes the opportunity of clarifying such matters to ensure that its data is properly interpreted and analysed. Contact should be made with the statistician responsible for the relevant subject matter. The CSO also has well-developed links with other national statistical services and with the statistical divisions of international organisations and will gladly advise researchers of appropriate contacts in such bodies.

The Role and Future Development of the Data Archive

DENISE LIEVESLEY

This paper describes the role of data archives from the perspectives of data users and data providers and it outlines the ways in which the role of archives is changing. The Data Archive at the University of Essex is used as an illustration of a social science archive in order to provide a backdrop against which the need for such a facility in the Republic of Ireland might be considered.

The growing importance of data archives

Data archives can have two distinct but interrelated activities: the preservation and the dissemination of data. Both functions have increased in importance over recent years.

There is an explosion of electronic data to be preserved but very limited expertise in their preservation. Specialist skills and equipment are needed to preserve electronic data to ensure they can still be used despite hardware and software changes. It thus makes sense to centralise the preservation of electronic material, or at the very least to build expertise in a central point from where it can be shared.

The increasing cost of data collection combined with the increasing concern about respondent burden means that collecting data afresh is seen as extravagant and attention has been focused on the use of secondary data. Related to this is an increasing recognition of the value of getting data used, particularly those data which have been collected using public funds or involving significant time on the part of respondents. There is also an increasing recognition of the importance of making research transparent and providing the opportunity for others to replicate or extend the analysis.

Data are inexhaustible and non-renewable and cannot be substituted: data cannot be exhausted no matter how much they are used; one person's use of the data does not diminish the data set in any way for the next use; once the chance to collect data has passed the potential data are lost forever; nothing other than data can serve the function of data. However there is a tension between data as a resource and data as a commodity. Whereas it is recognised that data are a public good and that *not* to use data incurs expense too, data sales raise badly needed revenue especially for official agencies whose budgets are under pressure.

International experience brought about in part by the use of the Internet for data exchange is changing the perspectives of both the data providers and the data users.

The Data Archive at the University of Essex

The Data Archive at the University of Essex was founded in 1967. It is funded by the Economic and Social Research Council (ESRC), the higher education funding councils and the University of Essex. It exists to promote wider and more informed use of data in teaching and research, and to preserve these data so that they continue to be accessible over time. It currently holds about 7,000 data sets of which approximately 4,500 are fully indexed. About 6,500 sets of data or documentation are distributed annually. Thus it has the dual roles of preservation and dissemination. The Archive's *raison d'être* is to promote the widest possible use of the data by providing a flexible and efficient user service and by sharing information and encouraging the use of data. The functions of the Archive are:

- establishing user needs
- acquisition
- validation
- documentation
- preservation
- cataloguing

- dissemination
- promotion
- user support.

Communities served by archives

Two distinct communities are served by archives: first, owners and funders, and second, users of data, particularly teachers and researchers.

Data providers

It is vital to retain the support of data providers. How can archives do this and what can they offer them? The benefits which can be offered to depositors are:

- preservation of and priority access to their own data
- promotion of the data by the encouragement of their wider use
- feedback on the use of data and the facilitation of a dialogue with users
- a buffer between the depositors and users if they wish, so that they are not troubled with user enquiries
- the citation of their data
- the kudos and honour of data acceptance
- value added to the data, for example by linking it to other data sets
- altruism, particularly if the data are useful in policy research and teaching
- contributing to creating a pool of better trained researchers
- maintenance of the control of the data
- financial return through sales of the data
- in some circumstances, purchase of the data.

The main sources of data are likely to be national and local government, other public bodies, quasi-autonomous non-governmental organisations and non-governmental organisations, individual academic researchers, academic centres, independent researchers, and the commercial sector including market research agencies.

The Data Archive at Essex has a special relationship with the ESRC which is, in my view, a good model for other funding councils within the UK and elsewhere to adopt. The ESRC corporate plan states that 'we will normally support effective information services rather than data set acquisition. We will only support acquisition if there is high demand, a cost effective mechanism for maintenance and support and perhaps a key leverage role for our support'. The ESRC data policy requires all grant recipients to offer the data they collect or acquire to the Data Archive for preservation and redistribution, and a proportion of the grants can be withheld until this happens. However grant applicants can include the costs required for data documentation and preparation as part of their funding requests. ESRC grant recipients are contacted very early in their research to alert them to this requirement and to work with them on ensuring they can comply. The issues addressed at that time include confidentiality, pledges to respondents, documentation standards and format.

The Archive's relationship with government departments is also very strong. Because of a lack of facilities for data preservation at the Public Record Office the Archive has become the de facto official archive for many of the government data sets.

Data users

The benefits to users are that they get access to information about data and publications, to the data themselves and to documentation. They have the opportunity to use data from different sources (from censuses, surveys and registers as well as from administrative sources) and the possibility to contact and work with other users and data producers.

There is an overemphasis on the use of published material with access to raw data often limited to a small number of privileged researchers. The advantages of sharing data, especially individual data in electronic form, are:

- to promote high standards of scientific enquiry
- to provide a common resource to permit the replication of research

- to permit the re-analysis of data often from a new perspective
- to facilitate the combination of data from multiple sources
- to exploit the existing resources rather than collecting new and expensive data.

Access to electronic data permits a level and depth of analysis which cannot be undertaken with published tabular material and permits analysts to verify, extend or elaborate upon the original results.

An acquisitions policy

Too much data are generated to make it feasible to accept all that is offered to an archive. Selection is essential and might take account of the views of potential users, the likely use now and in the future, whether data sets are in danger if not preserved, their importance as strategic, unique or influential data, and their relationship to other holdings (for example a data set might fill a gap or help to build specialist collections or alternatively might widen the holdings into new areas). On the other hand the rejection criteria might be: that the data are unlikely to be used, that the data are poor quality (though it is not clear what criteria would be used to judge this since quality is dependent upon the use to be made of the data), that there is inadequate documentation to describe the data, or that the data would be too expensive to acquire. A common reason for data not being obtained is that their availability might violate confidentiality pledges to respondents; although this is obviously an important issue, the problem is that the data may not be preserved for long-term access when confidentiality protection is no longer necessary.

As indicated above, quality is not absolute but is dependent upon the use. It is frequently defined as 'fitness for purpose'. The challenge is how data distributors can communicate information about the quality of data to users given that they have very different needs. A balance has to be achieved between improving and measuring quality and getting data out faster. One issue currently being addressed is the legal liability for distributing defective data.

Access to data

A balance must be achieved between respecting the demands of data providers in controlling access to data and taking advantage of developments such as the Internet. Resources need to be managed so that users for whom timeliness is critical get serviced as fast as possible but others are not neglected. In the commercial sector such rationing would be by charging but this is not necessarily available in the academic sector.

The Data Archive at Essex delivers data to users on media according to their need. The options include floppy disks, digital audio tapes, various cartridges, magnetic tapes, customised or mass-produced CD-ROMs as well as transferring data over the network. Some of the most frequently used data sets are mounted on the computer at the National Academic Computing Service based at Manchester University for on-line access. There is some flexibility over the software formats of data, with less frequently used formats requiring users to wait if they involve significant staff resources at the Archive. Similarly the Archive can produce extracts of data to users' specifications but a wait may be entailed.

The Archive's holdings are listed in an on-line catalogue called BIRON (Bibliographic retrieval on-line) which incorporates a standard study description for each data set plus text entered by a trained data cataloguer using a thesaurus. Catalogue searches can be made on topics, organisations, researchers, methodology, time or spatial characteristics, units of analysis, etc. Keyword searches and searches to identify the recent deposits in the Archive are also possible.

Data documentation

Documentation to describe data is crucial to ensure informed use of the data. It is best produced by depositors but they need persuasion, help and guidance. The format and media are important for ease of use and delivery. The preservation of documentation is also critical. Documentation can be a very valuable resource in its own right.

Data preservation

It is important that electronic data are preserved in a form which permits them to be accessible over time. The aims of preservation are to ensure that the physical reliability of data may be maintained, that security from unauthorised access is ensured and that the data continue to be accessible despite changes to the hardware and software environments. Technological developments permit the integration of data into preservation systems which also handle data information and management; this can be advantageous when several versions of a data set may be held and when data sets may be accessed with varying frequency, i.e. some data being used frequently and other data only very rarely.

The challenges for data preservation are:

- the growth in types of digital material along with the explosion of data quantity
- a wider range of data formats
- the poor acceptance of preservation standards
- the evolution of computer hardware
- the need to incorporate documentation
- the increase in data sets which are continually updated or may be corrected.

There have been developments in the reliability and longevity of storage media as well as improvements in optical storage and retrieval devices to enable better data management. Improved interfaces between software also assist in the transfer of data, and advances in data encryption techniques are assisting with version control and data security and auditing.

Developments at the Data Archive

The Data Archive at Essex has expanded to serve new communities by establishing a data service for access to historical data which have been made machine-readable, and by setting up, in conjunction with the University of Durham, a resource centre for access to data on Europe (known as R-Cade). Funding has been obtained from the European Community to enable us to embark on the first steps in a project to link the catalogues of the social science archives across Europe.

Developments are taking place to permit on-line access to data and documentation with visualisation, browsing and subsetting facilities. This can currently take place only with the depositor's permission but in future, when electronic security systems such as electronic signatures have been further developed and have gained legal acceptance, the potential of these facilities will be very great. One of the first steps is to ensure that documentation is in machine-readable form – which is currently a high priority either by scanning it or preferably by acquiring it in word-processed form – so that data and documentation may be linked and so that documentation may be used to a greater extent as a resource for teaching and research.

Conclusion

In this paper I have examined the advantages to data users and producers of the existence of a data archive which disseminates and preserves data. An archive devoted to social science data – current and perhaps also historical – is a valuable resource which will repay the investment many times over in terms of reducing the need for primary data collection and improving the skills and contribution of the research community. However the expertise and facilities required to run an effective preservation and dissemination programme for electronic material should not be underestimated. The time is ripe for Ireland to set up a facility for access to electronic material and, if this decision were made, the assistance of other national archives in sharing data and expertise would be forthcoming.

Nordic Archives and Electronic Records: Preservation of Electronic Records in Nordic Countries

MATTI PULKKINEN WITH TOM QUINLAN

Although politically and linguistically distinct, Nordic countries[1] share common characteristics: all are small nations, with population sizes ranging from Iceland's approximate 260,000 inhabitants to Sweden's 8,700,000; and, although no longer especially religious countries, all share common social values which have a basis in Lutheranism and this Lutheran heritage can now be seen in the role of the state within society. It is perhaps in the legal systems of Nordic countries that the influence of Lutheranism on the role of the state is most discernible, with legislative provisions which respect the rights of the individual citizen. Such laws have had important implications for the preservation of archives and for access to information: all of the Nordic countries have legislation to ensure the preservation of the archives of government agencies because of their legal, evidential and research value, and to guarantee the individual citizen freedom of access to the information contained in the records of government agencies. In addition, there are strong privacy laws to ensure that access to and disclosure of personal information, especially that which is created and stored electronically, does not violate the privacy of the individual.

The respective national archives of the five Nordic countries are responsible primarily for the preservation of records created by the functioning of government agencies and this naturally includes responsibility for those records created and stored in electronic format. Preservation of electronic records began about two decades ago in some of the Scandinavian countries within the Nordic group and it is expected that, in common with many other archival repositories throughout the world, all of the Nordic national repositories will in future have to administer increasingly large holdings of archival information in electronic format. Since the 1970s, the Danish and Swedish national archival repositories have preserved the electronic archives of government agencies. The National Archives of Denmark has about 3,000 reels of electronic records, but, to date, these records have not been used very often and then usually only by a small number of individual research projects. The National Archives of Sweden has some 11,000 to 12,000 reels of records in electronic format and about 3,480 cassettes. The National Archives of Norway first accessioned electronic records in 1985 and currently has approximately 500 reels. Until 1995, both the Finnish and the Icelandic national archives contracted out the function of physically preserving electronic archives to computer centres. However, this arrangement was found to be unsatisfactory. In the case of the National Archives of Finland, it was observed that preservation criteria were met only from a technical and not from an archival point of view. The Finnish State Computer Centre, the organisation to which the task of preserving government records in electronic format was entrusted, was capable of providing a safe repository and it possessed the necessary equipment to migrate the information to new storage media and to preserve it intact. Also, the State Computer Centre was, to a certain extent, able to preserve the records in a manner that safeguarded the legal and evidential value of the information. However, it was considered that researcher access under this arrangement did not compare satisfactorily with that for hardcopy archives, and there were also problems in ensuring that well-organised system documentation and inventories were preserved. From 1996 both the National Archives of Finland and the National Archives of Iceland will themselves assume direct responsibility for all aspects of the preservation of the archives of government agencies which are in electronic format.

The national archival repositories in the Scandinavian countries which have been carrying out aspects of preserving the electronic archives of government agencies require that permanent computer records be transferred to them in a hardware- and software-independent format. Transferred files must be written in 8-bit

ASCII or EBCDIC (flat files) and be delivered on traditional $^1/_2$ inch magnetic tape (9-track open reel). These storage media use a standardised and system-independent data structure. They are, however, losing ground among mainframes and have been rarely used in PC environments. It has therefore proved necessary for Nordic national archival repositories, in common with other repositories of electronic archives, to seek alternative storage media for future transfers of electronic records. When computer archives are delivered by government agencies, their readability and compliance with the agencies' system documentation is tested. Documentation sufficient to support secondary analysis must accompany the computer records when they are transferred for archival preservation. This documentation must contain identification and definition of all data sets, length and definition of all data elements (records and fields) and code books for all unique codes used in the records. Documentation of this type may be called metadata (data about data).

In addition to the national archival repositories, there are organisations within Nordic countries which were established specifically to preserve data in electronic format. The Danish Data Archives is a national data bank and documentation and technical service facility for researchers and students. It is an independent unit within the Danish state archives service. The Norwegian Social Science Data Service was established in 1971 by the Norwegian Research Council to serve the needs of the social science research community. Its main function is to develop databases and relevant software to secure easy access to empirical data. The Swedish Social Science Data Service, located at Göteborg University, is the Swedish data archive for machine-readable data in the social sciences and the humanities. Neither Finland nor Iceland has a dedicated data archives.

It should be borne in mind that there are fundamental differences between the data archive function as currently performed in the Scandinavian countries and the practice of their national archival repositories in preserving government archives. Data archives store anonymous data and this makes it possible to give access to this information without violating the privacy of the individual. However, archival repositories cannot always depersonalise the material of which they have custody. Records such as censuses must be preserved with all details, and more stringent security requirements must be in place to balance the requirement of providing access to information with protecting the privacy of the individual. This means that the level of access to information held by data archives can often be greater than in the case of the national archival repositories preserving the archives of government agencies, and data archives are generally perceived to serve the demands of scientific studies extremely well. This has certainly been the experience of Denmark, Norway and Sweden. In Finland and Iceland, where there are no separate data archives, and in the Scandinavian countries, the national archival repositories could not provide the same level of service that data archives can. Compliance with privacy legislation can cause problems for the national archival repositories in providing access to records which have been appraised for permanent preservation. The need to ensure that the privacy of individuals to which records relate is not violated can often result in information having to be kept secret until all such persons have died. Although inconvenient for research purposes, especially in the social sciences, such a situation is preferable to the alternative of having the records of a government agency destroyed because of privacy considerations, as such a practice would inevitably lead one to question if such a form of *ethical appraisal* was not actually censorship. It is essential that the integrity of an archival repository in preserving information can be relied upon, and this can often entail access to information being strictly controlled and even denied. This requirement can often hamper the access to electronic information that is so readily provided by a data archives.

In addition, freedom of information legislation can have implications which are peculiar to electronic archives. Freedom of information legislation in Nordic countries decrees that all of the records of a government agency are open to public inspection unless they contain categories of information which are specifically exempt. Such exemptions can include, for example, medical files or the records of a government's foreign ministry. This means that a government agency must have a valid legal reason for denying a member of the public access to information contained in its records. Freedom of information laws naturally apply to the information contained in electronic records too. However, in contrast to conventional records, compliance with the legislation can be more difficult where electronic records are concerned. It can be quite difficult to define where there is a public record in an informational system. Is it a data file on a hard disk? Is it a combination of records to be seen on the computer's VDU?

Notes

1   Denmark, Finland, Iceland, Norway and Sweden. 'Nordic' is not a synonym for 'Scandinavian': Finland and Iceland are not Scandinavian countries. In Denmark, Iceland, Norway and Sweden and in some parts of Finland, Germanic languages are spoken. However, Finnish, the language of the majority of Finns, is a Finno-Urgic language.

Organisations preserving electronic information in Nordic countries

Denmark
: National Archives of Denmark (*Rigsarkivet*), Riksdagsgarden 9, DK–1218, Copenhagen, Denmark. Tel +45–33–92 33 10

  Danish Data Archives (*Dansk Data Arkivet*), Islandsgade 10, DK–5000, Odense C., Denmark. Tel +45–66–11 30 10

Finland
: National Archives of Finland (*Kansallisarkisto*), Rauhankatu 17, PO Box 258, FIN–00171, Helsinki, Finland

Iceland
: National Archives of Iceland (*Islands Nationalarkivet*), Postholv R5–5390 105, Reykjavik, Iceland. Tel +354–56–23 393

Norway
: National Archives of Norway (*Riksarkivet*), Postboks 10, Kringsjo N–0807, Oslo, Norway. Tel +47–22–0 22 600

  Norwegian Social Science Data Services (*Nodsk Samfunnsvitskapleg datateneste*), Hans Holmboes g. 22, Bergen 5007, Norway. Tel. +47–55–21 2117

Sweden   National Archives of Sweden (*Riksarkivet*),
Fyrverkarbacken 13, PO Box 12541, Stockholm
S–10229, Sweden. Tel +46–8–737 6350

Swedish Social Science Data Service (*Svensk
Samhallsvetenkaplig Datatjanst*), Göteborg
University, Pilgatan 19A, Göteborg 411 22, Sweden.
Tel +46–31–773 1210

Social Science Data Archives in the New World?

ANNE GILLILAND-SWETLAND

Introduction

I was asked to talk about North American aspects of social science data archives, but as I thought more about this paper and my own background, I decided that what distinguishes the American from the European data archives environment is probably more a matter of degree than of substance – North America has been maintaining social science data archives longer than many other countries and so its archives have in many cases more substantial holdings in a wider range of computer media and formats to a larger and more diverse set of users. Additionally, emerging computer network and multimedia technologies have been adopted particularly quickly by researchers at American academic institutions for the creation and manipulation of data sets. North American data archives are having to cope not only with users whose needs range from the most traditional to the most cutting-edge, but also with the preservation, validation and dissemination of several decades of data that are growing increasingly voluminous and multidimensional.

This paper, therefore, will expand its focus from the national to the international, even the global scene, and attempt to give some overview of the place of data archives in the global information infrastructure. This is in part because these are the areas in which my knowledge and work are primarily based. In larger part, however, it is because there is a need for social science data archives to build strategic partnerships and structures that will help them to grapple with interacting technological, economic and disciplinary trends that are occurring on a worldwide, interprofessional and interdisciplinary basis. This new world of the global information infrastructure has major implications not only for data identification, accessioning, validation, preservation, description, delivery and demand, but also for data discovery and augmentation.

I will give a brief overview of what I see to be some of the opportunities and challenges facing today's data archives, and there are two questions in particular that I hope the paper will provoke. Firstly, in this new world, this emerging global information infrastructure of such enormous vision and enterprise and yet enormous disparities, is there still a distinct role or set of roles that social science data archives can play in America or internationally? Secondly, if the answer to this first question is 'yes', as I hope it is, what are those roles most likely to be?

Background

Despite the facts that electronic records management is receiving considerable attention in US and Canadian archival education and literature, and that several high profile law suits have drawn news media attention to the topic, archival electronic records programs in organisational settings are still in fledgling states in most institutions (with a few government agencies, most notably the National Archives and Records Administration and the New York State Archives and Records Administration, well out in front). This is not the case with social science data archives, which in North America generally exist as separate entities from organisational or 'traditional' archives, although both frequently coexist within the same institutions, especially in academic settings. Social science data archives have been the flagships of data management in the US for many years, pioneering in both the preservation and the use of what used to be referred to as machine-readable records and today are more likely to be called digital data sets.

In the period following World War II, as the social science disciplines began to develop and academia began to realise that the data processing potential of computers that had been envisioned by luminaries such as Vannevar Bush might actually become a reality, North America played a pioneering role in pulling these two trends together into a new concept – the social science data archives. Two of the earliest American social science data archives have become particularly prominent and illustrate well contemporary structures and functions of social science data archives. One of these is the Roper Center for Public Opinion Research at the University of

Connecticut. The Roper Center, established shortly after the end of the war, is the repository for Roper, Gallup and other major public opinion polls and serves as the world's largest public opinion library. The second is the Inter-university Consortium for Political and Social Research (ICPSR) based at the University of Michigan. ICPSR, established almost thirty-five years ago, serves both as a data repository and as a consortium of several hundred member sites worldwide. Most of those member sites are colleges and universities, and several of them maintain their own prominent data libraries, for example Columbia University's Electronic Data Service, Virginia University's Social Sciences Data Center and the University of Wisconsin's Data and Program Library Service. ICPSR's administrative structure is run largely through membership dues, and it circulates its holdings in a variety of formats and media to other data libraries or ICPSR's own representatives at member sites. These representatives are then able to assist remote users who requested data sets to mount and use them.

In general, the primary roles that North American data archives and data libraries have performed in the last several decades have been to preserve and validate large quantities of social science research data for subsequent reuse; to make this research data available in computer-manipulable, and in the past, predominantly software-independent form; and to train users in quantitative data analysis techniques and software. One indication of the future and how these roles might evolve, or at least broaden into a wider facilitative information structure, began to be seen in the 1980s with the end of the Cold War and increased accessibility of the Internet to researchers for international communication. Users were hungry for data exchange between countries and for the capability to compare data across countries. The US also wished to redeploy Cold War scientists and put their skills to work in new research areas. One area singled out was environmental research, especially the study of global warming, and this resulted in the establishment of the Consortium for International Earth Science Information Network, or CIESIN, which is based in Saginaw, Michigan. CIESIN is an illustration of an upgraded model for data archives, not only because it is interdisciplinary (with both a science and a social science focus) and international in scope, but because a massive amount of its holdings and those of other consortium members comprises software-dependent spatial data associated metadata. CIESIN also provides a World Wide Web environment that encourages user data discovery and access to metadata and related socioeconomic, social science and natural science information resources held at other sites around the world. Such an environment assists users in augmenting the data supplied by CIESIN through cross-compilation with data from other sources and also facilitates data visualisation. CIESIN has developed a structure called an 'Information Co-operative' whereby CIESIN partners around the world operate local computer servers or 'nodes' that are able to provide a distributed environment for mounting, visualising and analysing data, as well as browsing other information resources.

In the 1990s, North American social science data archives face unprecedented challenges and expansion potential due to techno-logical, economic and disciplinary trends, and escalating demand for their data. Partly driving these trends and demand is the way that data, information and knowledge (however one may choose to define those terms) are already being treated as commodities in an increasingly entrepreneurial, digitally networked globe. This globe is spanned by an Internet that is no longer dominated by academic and research interests, but, since early 1995, has been partly run by and available for commercial use. The burgeoning use of the World Wide Web as a hypermedia information delivery system bears evi-dence to these developments. Many new and potentially rival information providers, some in the commercial sector, some devel-oping so-called digital or electronic libraries and archives, are becoming involved in the creation, location, delivery and packaging of non-bibliographic data. These new information providers bring a considerable amount of technological sophistication to the devel-opment of networked digital environments that can disseminate research data of all types, including the capability to link data to other materials such as published sources, images and maps. Such information providers, however, are not necessarily fully aware of or considering the complexities and policy issues associated with preserving and accessing existing and new data sets over time.

Traditional organisational archivists, as I mentioned earlier, are also moving into electronic records management. These archivists are recognising that their profession and theoretical constructs can play key roles in the appraisal, description and preservation of digital materials. Indeed, the Society of American Archivists has had a recommended postgraduate education curriculum for electronic records education in place for about three years now and is pushing for all US archivists to be educated in the management of electronic records by the end of the decade. In the case of the college and university archivists, however, who now represent the largest segment of the US archival profession, and who frequently collect faculty members' research papers as well as the institution's administrative papers, there is the possibility of yet another overlap in functions with the social science data archives. Or, to put a more positive spin on this, there is perhaps a real opportunity for partnerships and resource-sharing in the post-custodial archival world.

The development and use of networked information technologies enjoy a strong symbiotic relationship with economic factors. The financial realities associated with acquiring and maintaining technology by researchers; the conducting of large-scale studies where major government funding agencies such as the National Endowment for the Humanities and the Department of Education are experiencing massive cuts in their own appropriations; and the survival of academic disciplines in a time of much straitened US college and university resources for the arts, humanities and social sciences have all pushed researchers towards more large-scale collaborative research. The development of readily accessible and easy to use computer networks and software has both facilitated this collaboration and led to more sophisticated and multimedia data sets being created. At the same time, however, disparities have increased between social science data archives users in terms of their technological capabilities and expectations. While all this has been occurring, the social science disciplines themselves have continued to evolve and to become more interdisciplinary and international in scope. There is also increased use of social science research methodologies and computers in the humanities and more instances of scholarly research that bring together researchers in the sciences with those in the social sciences, humanities, even the arts. It is hard, however, to predict what the impact of computers will eventually be, not only upon how research is conducted within these disciplines, but even upon how these disciplines conceive of themselves and their objects of study.

I would like to turn now to some questions that are raised by specific changes that are occurring.

New dimensions in the data themselves

The research materials being created today that data archives are supposed ultimately to manage are changing in dimensionality, scope and volume. We are now in the era of multidimensional data created by Geographic Information Systems (e.g., remotely sensed, historical mapping, urban geography or anthropology applications), object-oriented databases, hypermedia and multimedia, even virtual reality research environments, that cannot be retained in software-independent (or flat) formats and with which archivists need to be involved from the moment of creation if they are going to have a hope of managing them. There is also a growing realisation among users and data archivists alike that the contextual information (closely allied to the evidential content sought after by traditional archivists) is also valuable for immediate and subsequent data analysis, but very hard to preserve.

What are the challenges posed by these new dimensions in data? They include the massive volume of the materials to be managed, the wide bandwidth that will be required for dissemination of the data, the need for standard data migration paths to ensure the ultimate usability of software-dependent data with its evidence intact and, last but far from least, privacy. Illustrating the importance of this latter point, Richard Rockwell, Executive Director of ICPSR, warned as long ago as 1992 that while:

> ICPSR has always been committed to preserving the anonymity of survey respondents . . . The problem is that some new datasets challenge our previous methods of abiding by our commitment to confidentiality. 'Contextual' data, for instance, which provides aggregate information on the area in which a respondent lives as well as the respondent's responses to survey questions, may make it theoretically possible to re-identify the respondent.

Fortunately, multiple strategies are emerging that address the changing nature of digital data. For example, data archivists can heighten their proactivity in assisting researchers in creating software-dependent data sets that utilise standard operating platforms and data exchange protocols, thus making the ultimate migration path less tricky. By the same measure, by becoming involved at the front end of standards development, data archivists can work to ensure that other engaged communities are aware of the long-term preservation and access issues that need to be considered. (Here there is a strong communality of interest with organisational archivists who are also interested in using standards to ensure interoperability, development and preservation of appropriate and sufficient metadata, long-term viability of storage media and the development of predictable and searchable data structures (SGML).) The issue of privacy in the electronic data world and how it balances against freedom of information is a difficult one, but one that archivists understand well. Some help may come here from commercial interests working on the development of data encryption and security protocols for on-line financial transactions (or electronic commerce). Another tack, suggested by ICPSR, is that a data archives might provide a service that would be queried remotely by users and would give results only to the question asked, instead of distributing directly to the user a copy of all the contextual information that is included in a data set.

New dimensions in delivery mechanisms

We are seeing a whole range of delivery mechanisms for digital data, including diskette, tape, 3480 and 8 mm tape cartridges and CD-ROM for off-line data delivery, and FTP, gopher and World Wide Web for on-line. The World Wide Web, as probably the newest of these delivery mechanisms, can serve a range of functions – delivering data and scanned versions of associated documentation; facilitating indexed access to databases and metadata; and providing links to other Internet sites, individuals through e-mail, library catalogs, even glossaries and full text of published secondary materials. Networks give us the potential, with bandwidth limitations, of delivering the same data simultaneously to multiple users or collaborators across time and space, and to share data processing of large files – a convenient way to respond to burgeoning user demand for data and CPU space without putting more pressure on data archives staff for physical tape retrieval and mailing. This diversity of options, however, brings with it another host of questions, for example:

- How to fund conversion to new delivery media for users with high end technological capabilities and still continue to provide full services to users with lower levels of technological facilities or skills?

- Issues of user training and how best to deliver documentation, especially if one moves to unmediated access. North American archives are increasingly moving to OCRed or bitmapped versions of documentation, for example, but is it enough just to give these to the users, or will they need additional assistance? What happens if we use the networks to deliver data directly to users who are at home or in the field or otherwise not close to a campus data archives representative?

- What other mechanisms, such as object-oriented programs, need to be developed for indexing or otherwise rendering code books searchable, and could such tools be standardised for use across data repositories?

- What is the data archives going to give up, if it adds on these new services? What new revenue stream might come into play to support an additional layer of services? Is this a growing phase that will pass over time and old services can be dropped, or is one of our roles actually to support all these changes? Do we need to accept that integrating/facilitating dynamism and multilevel needs is a permanent fact of life?

- Finally, can development costs be shared with other data providers?

New data creators and providers

In this new world, everyone can become a publisher, and increasingly the creators themselves, be they individual researchers or national governments, are putting their own data up on-line. In the US, as in many other national government settings, federal and state government agencies are being encouraged to deliver the information they collect directly on-line to the public as part of a movement towards increased government efficiency and accessibility. Government data sets are also being sold to commercial developers who then repackage or otherwise add value to the data and sell it to the consumer. Digital or electronic libraries and archives, some growing out of geography or engineering disciplines, some in major research libraries, facilitate moving transparently in one digital environment between published literature and underlying empirical data, allowing users to replicate studies and experiments, recompile data in new ways, even upload their own annotations to the data sets. In light of such developments, do existing models for data archives still hold good, and what services do they perform? One potential role for archives in general in this potential chaos of information providers was that identified in a recent report by the Commission on Preservation and Access and the Research Libraries Group. This report suggested that archives might serve as certified repositories that could guarantee the validity and long-term preservation of data and assist users in identifying quality, trustworthy information.

Conclusion

I return to my opening questions. Will there be a role for data archives in North America, and indeed in the new world? That depends upon how well data archives understand and articulate their particular contribution in this global information infrastructure, and how well they work together. Strategic partnerships definitely seem at the moment to be the way of the future. In 1992, Richard Rockwell was asking questions about how to facilitate the growing need to be able to analyse international events and trends where the data required fell beyond the scope of one repository.

> Which non-US datasets could and should ICPSR acquire
> for its members? What priority should be given to acquiring non-US data? To what extent should ICPSR rely on data

archives in other countries to make needed datasets available to ICPSR members? And, finally, is the concept of an 'international data co-operative' feasible in a world with Internet connectivity but with legal and political barriers to transmittal of information?

ICPSR, CIESIN and so many other North American social science data archives that are accessible over the Internet and are actively involved in consortia and co-operative relationships have already proved to us that the 'international data co-operative' is not only feasible but desirable. So what should the role of data archives be in this new world? It may seem obvious to state it to this audience, but the preservation of massive volumes of digital data for long-term access and recompilation and secondary analysis, and all the associated policy, validation and standards issues, are areas where data archivists, and archivists in general, are especially skilled and experienced. Unfortunately, this may not be quite so readily apparent to others moving into the business, at least until chaos develops. In the next decade, social science data archives in America could play a vital role catering to users at multiple levels, providing data validation/certification and data preservation over time. This will only happen, however, if data archives take full advantage of every opportunity to influence information technology standards and national policy development, as well as the structures that allow us to link our holdings to those of others.

References

Commission on Preservation and Access and the Research Libraries Group, *Report of the Task Force on the Archiving of Digital Information*, 1995

Dogan, Matei, 'Fragmentation of the Social Sciences and Recombination of Specialities Around Sociology', *International Social Science Journal*, 46, 1 (Feb. 1994), pp. 27–42

Inter-university Consortium for Political and Social Research, *Annual Report, 1991–1992*, ICPSR, Ann Arbor, MI, c.1993

Scheuch, Erwin K., 'From a Data Archive to an Infrastructure for the Social Sciences', *International Social Science Journal*, 42 (Feb. 1990), pp. 93–111

Electronic Records in the US Federal Government: One Archivist's Perspective[1]

MARK CONRAD

In this paper I want to give some background information about how the US federal government has traditionally managed its electronic records. I then want to look at one type of electronic records – e-mail messages – to illustrate some of the challenges that new record types are posing to the traditional records management practices. Then I want to deal briefly with some federal initiatives to answer these challenges.

First I want to set the stage by discussing some of the legislation that has an impact on the management of federal records. The definition of a federal record found in the Federal Records Act of 1951, as amended, includes records in all formats. Electronic records do fall within the definition of a federal record.[2]

Under Chapter 31 of Title 44 of the United States Code, the head of each federal agency is required to 'make and preserve records containing adequate and proper documentation of the organization, functions, policies, decisions, procedures, and essential transactions of the agency and designed to furnish the information necessary to protect the legal and financial rights of the Government and of persons directly affected by the agency's actions'. Agencies are also required to manage their records. The head of each agency has to appoint a person that is responsible for ensuring the agency meets its records management requirements. This person is usually the primary point of contact with the National Archives.

Under Chapter 33 of Title 44, the head of each government agency must schedule the final disposition of the agency's records with the National Archives. No agency can dispose of records without the approval of the Archivist of the United States.

Records scheduled for permanent retention because of their legal, evidential or informational value are normally transferred to the National Archives when they are no longer needed for agency business. In the case of electronic records, the National Archives will often negotiate with federal agencies to obtain a copy of the records while they are still in use.

The Center for Electronic Records is the unit within the National Archives that is responsible for the appraisal, accessioning, preservation, description and reference services of the electronic records of the federal government. There are other units within the National Archives that have some electronic records responsibilities, but the Center for Electronic Records carries out the basic archival functions of identifying records that should be permanently retained, preserving those records and providing access to them.

I now want to outline my view of the 'traditional' model of electronic records practice in the federal government. This is a very broad brush model. I do not want to get bogged down in the details of how electronic records are handled. The procedures for handling electronic records are constantly revised to reflect changes in technology and users' needs, but in general terms this is what happens.

An agency creates some electronic records using their electronic information systems. The agency contacts the National Archives to propose the final disposition of the records.

An archivist from the Center for Electronic Records is sent to examine the records in their native environment – that is, in the system or systems in which they were created, manipulated and stored. The archivist determines whether or not the records have sufficient legal, evidential or informational value to warrant their permanent retention.

If the records have sufficient value to warrant their long-term retention the National Archives arranges for the transfer of the records from the agency to the National Archives. Under current federal regulations, agencies are required to transfer records to the National Archives in a hardware- and software-independent format – ASCII or EBCDIC – and on prescribed media – 3480 cartridges, $^1/_2$ inch open-reel tapes or CD-ROMs.

When the records arrive at the Center for Electronic Records, they are checked to make sure the records are what the agency claims to have sent; to make sure that there is sufficient information about the data to understand how the records were created and used; and to make sure the records are readable.

If the records pass all these checks, two copies of the records are made on the current 'archival' medium of choice. The Center is using 3480 cartridges at present for this purpose. No current medium can be considered a 'permanent' medium. All electronic records will have to be moved to new media over time because the technology used to store records on current media will become obsolete.

Once the two copies have been made they are stored at separate locations under tight temperature and humidity control. The Center tests a statistically significant sample of the tapes on an annual basis to identify any data losses. If any data loss is detected the Center attempts to discover its cause and correct it. All other tapes that might have been affected by the same cause are also read and corrected if possible. All records are copied to new media at least once every ten years.[3]

Once the electronic records have been accessioned, they are described. The Center for Electronic Records produces a variety of finding aids to its holdings. Some of these finding aids are available on the Internet.[4]

Until very recently a researcher interested in using electronic records from the Center's holdings had very few options. The researcher could examine hard-copy finding aids and documentation for the records. If the researcher decided that a particular set of records might be of interest, the Center would provide the researcher with tapes containing the records and copies of the documentation on a cost recovery basis. The researcher had to take the tapes and use them on computers elsewhere.

The Center now provides access to a limited number of data sets in the research room. The Center hopes to expand its repertoire of reference services further in the near future.

That is my view of the traditional model for archival electronic records practice in the US federal government. When this model first came into use most of the records the Center for Electronic Records was accessioning were statistical data sets or files from simple database applications. This model worked fairly well for these types of records.

Today, however, the federal government is using computers to produce a greater variety of increasingly complex electronic records. Relational and object-oriented database management systems, Geographic Information Systems, electronic mail systems, executive information systems and other types of computer applications all produce electronic records that pose new challenges to the traditional model.

I want to look at records created by e-mail systems to illustrate some of these challenges. One of the problems is the volume of records created by e-mail systems. It is enormous. One system that I am acquainted with which has a relatively small number of users produces over 32,000 messages per week. Not all of those messages are records. Some are personal communications. Some are records with only short-term value. Others, however, have been appraised as having permanent value.

The volume of records poses a number of challenges. The number of e-mail systems that are producing records keeps growing. If all the agencies tried to schedule the disposition of their e-mail records at once, the Center's staff would be overwhelmed. The archivists have to be able to get the big picture. They have to have an understanding of what systems are out there and what purposes they are used for so that they can prioritise their appraisal.

Another problem is that most e-mail systems are not designed to hold records for an extended period of time. A decision has to be made quickly about what to do with the records or the system will become overloaded. The ideal situation would be to have disposition decisions made before the first record is created.

Obviously you cannot schedule and appraise individual messages. You have to be able to systematically sort the 'wheat' from the 'chaff'. This leads us to our next challenge – separating records with permanent value from temporary records and non-record material.

Most e-mail systems do not include archival or records management functionality. They do not provide tools for easily isolating and preserving records with lasting value. Another problem is that many users of e-mail systems do not understand their record-keeping responsibilities. Until recently many federal workers did not understand that when they used e-mail to conduct official business, they were creating federal records. Many agencies have not implemented filing procedures or other methods of ensuring the proper disposition of their e-mail records.

Another challenge is capturing all the components of an e-mail message that make up an electronic record. You have to be able to capture the content, context and structure of the electronic record. This is not as easy as it sounds. For example, e-mail messages often contain cryptic acronyms for the addressees. Some of my mail comes to 'C4L'. Fifty years from now who will know who C4L was? You need to know the full names and titles of the senders and recipients of messages. It may be important to know if the recipient of a message actually read the message, but this information is not routinely captured with the text of the message. Some systems allow users to forward mail or reply to messages and include the full text of the original message. It is important to be able to tell where one message ends and the next begins! Then, you have to be able to move all that information to new computers and software when the 'current' software and hardware become obsolete.

The arrangement of the records presents another challenge. The records are usually not stored in the e-mail system in the way that they are presented to users. They are often stored in the order in which they are created or received. Yet how the messages appeared to the individual user may provide a great deal of context for that message. Was the message about your pay rise one of several hundred in a giant folder where it could never be found and read, or was it in a folder marked 'extremely urgent handle at once'? This may be very important contextual information.

Another problem is that key elements of a message may be almost inextricably intertwined with the e-mail system software. Information about who read what message when may only be stored in a system file. Other elements of a message may be created in a format that cannot be reduced to a standard format such as ASCII. Graphic, audio and video attachments to e-mail often cannot easily be moved from the software that they were created in – but that software will eventually become obsolete.

The last challenge that I will mention is providing researcher access to e-mail records. Obviously, a researcher interested in how a particular project was handled by a particular office does not want to acquire a copy of all the e-mail messages created by that agency during the two years that the project was running. You have to be able to locate messages that are relevant to that person's inquiry and make them available in a usable form.

You also have to be able to screen all the messages before you hand them over to the researcher. The records may contain information that cannot be released. For example, they may contain information that would raise security or personal privacy concerns. If there are only five or six messages of interest to the researcher, they could probably be screened individually. If, on the other hand, there are several thousand messages it would be a much more difficult task.

There, in brief, are some of the challenges today's electronic records pose to the federal government's traditional model for handling them. I would like now to mention some of the initiatives that are under way that should help address some of these challenges.

The Government Information Locator System, or GILS, is designed to help the public find out about, and gain access to, information created or received by the federal government. Agencies of the federal government must post information about their information products and services on the Internet. More importantly from an archival point of view, they also have to post information about all their electronic information systems that contain electronic records. The National Archives helped shape the final form of the GILS. The information that the agencies will have to post should help the Archives to prioritise appraisal. Appraisal archivists will be able to get the big picture of what records are being created and need to be scheduled by examining the posted information.

The National Archives recently issued guidance on the management of e-mail records. The guidance clarifies agency responsibility for managing e-mail records. It also identifies the key elements of an e-mail message that must be preserved in order to preserve an e-mail record. This guidance has been widely distributed and I believe is still available on the National Archives World Wide Web site.

Various units within the National Archives are working with agencies to help them come up with reasonable solutions for implementing their record-keeping requirements. In some cases this means agencies will print out the text of e-mail messages, record other relevant contextual information on paper and file the information in the appropriate hard-copy files. Other agencies are developing electronic record-keeping systems for their electronic records. The National Archives is working with both groups.

Personnel from the Center for Electronic Records and other units of the Archives have been involved in a number of projects to try to incorporate archival and records management functionality into new electronic information systems. One of the expected outcomes of these projects is that it will be easier to identify, preserve and provide access to the electronic records that have lasting value.

The Department of Defense is trying to take this concept one step further. In January 1995 it established the Department of Defense Records Management Task Force for a period of one year. According to the 'Task Force Direction' statement found on the Task Force World Wide Web home page:

> The DoD records management vision is to meet future needs by managing information as records, in a cost-effective manner, in any medium, throughout its life-cycle. A primary goal of the task force is to initiate change in DoD records management processes. These changes will meet mission needs, assure compliance with federal records management standards, improve records management functions, and allow successful management planning. The task force is the focal point for co-ordinating many DoD efforts.[5]

This task force is headed by the Director of the Center for Electronic Records.

Personnel from the Center and other organisations are trying to define metadata standards for e-mail. The idea is to come up with a standard way to record the content, context and structure of an e-mail message so that an e-mail record can easily be moved to new computer systems as the older systems become obsolete. A number of organisations within the federal government, including the Center, are also looking for solutions to the problem of finding messages that meet a researcher's needs from amidst the untold numbers of electronic records created by e-mail and other text-based systems. If metadata standards for e-mail can be developed, they may provide paths for easier access to individual messages.

Those are just a few of the initiatives that are currently under way in the federal government in an effort to meet the challenges which electronic records continue to pose for information management, for records management and for archival services. The US federal government is trying to meet those challenges, and the National Archives and Records Administration is an important participant in this effort.

My own experience with electronic records has led me to several conclusions. I strongly believe that in the world of electronic records there is no substitute for practical experience. You cannot begin to understand the full dimensions of the challenges electronic records pose until you try to implement solutions to some of those challenges.

Institutions worldwide face similar challenges; I believe it is important that information is shared across boundaries whether those boundaries are national or professional. There are too many problems to be addressed. We cannot afford duplication of effort. The problems we face are very complex. It will take a team approach to meet the challenges.

The time to act is now. The challenges will not go away, but if we do not act quickly important records will.

Notes

1 I wish to make it abundantly clear that the views expressed here are my own views. While my perspective has been informed by my work at the US National Archives and at University College Dublin, I do not speak for either institution. All statements, opinions and conjectures are my own unless otherwise attributed.
2 Federal records, as defined in 44 U.S.C. 3301, include all books, papers, maps, photographs, machine-readable materials, or other documentary materials, regardless of physical form or characteristics, made or received by an agency of the United States government under federal law or in connection with the transaction of public business and preserved or appropriate for preservation by that agency or its legitimate successor as evidence of the organisation, functions, policies, decisions, procedures, operations, or other activities of the government or

because of the informational value of data in them. Library and museum material made or acquired and preserved solely for reference or exhibition purposes, extra copies of documents preserved only for the convenience of reference, and stocks of publications and of processed documents are not included.

3 For more information about the preservation procedures used by the Center for Electronic Records see Chapter 12 of Title 36 of the United States Code of Federal Regulations. Each year Center staff draw a random sample of 384 tapes and check them for data loss. This sample gives the Center a 98 per cent confidence level of finding errors which occur in 1 per cent of the records.

4 These finding aids can currently be found by pointing a World Wide Web browser to the National Archives and Records Administration's home page at: http://www.nara.gov

5 This statement was found by pointing a World Wide Web browser at the URL: http://www.dtic.dla.mil/c3i/recmgmt.html

An Irish Social Science Data Archive: Prospect and Problems

BRENDAN J. WHELAN

The nature and functions of data archives

Definition

Social science data archives are repositories of electronically read-able information on topics of interest to social scientists. Such archives now exist in most European countries and form a valu-able resource for the social science community. Some steps have recently been taken at European level to co-ordinate and develop these institutions (e.g. the Large Scale Facilities initiative from DG XII of the European Commission and the Luxembourg Income Study initiative). Social science in this context is interpreted very broadly to include not just sociology but also all sciences con-cerned with human populations such as economics and business studies, psychology, political science, aspects of medicine and geography.

Modern data processing technology has changed the manner in which archives operate. Some years ago, the structure and format of most social science data, and the media on which they were stored, militated against easy accessibility and transferability. With the advent of generally available packages such as SPSS and SAS, which have the capacity to produce self-documenting files, the busi-ness of storing, retrieving and documenting social science data sets has become more routine. The universal availability of new media such as optical disks, DAT-type tape cassettes and data compression software for PC diskettes has also facilitated these processes. Indeed, it would be possible to envisage an archive operating nowadays on a 'virtual' basis, i.e. maintaining a complete and up-to-date cata-logue giving full documentation on each data set but without holding the data themselves. The latter would be available from the owner institution in a standardised and agreed format.

Content

It would probably be fair to say that in their early days archives tended to concentrate on survey data sets. More recently, the range of information held has expanded considerably, and in several countries such as the UK the national office of statistics routinely makes the results and data sets for important inquiries available to social scientists through the national data archive.

The types of information held in social science archives may be characterised as follows:

1. published data in electronically accessible form such as the information held in the Central Statistics Office's EOLAS data bank

2. more detailed breakdowns of published data such as the small area population statistics (SAPS) derived from the census

3. primary data sets such as the individual responses to surveys conducted by the national statistical office (e.g. the Labour Force Survey), universities, research institutes, market research companies etc. Some of these surveys are of a once-off kind and others may be carried out on a regular basis.

Benefits of data archives

Social scientists find archives increasingly important. First, social science data are very expensive to collect and it is vital that the data collected be utilised as fully as possible. Typically, researchers collect much more data than are published in any given study: the archive gives others the chance to exploit the full range of data collected. Secondly, the existence of archives encourages researchers to replicate and re-analyse previous work (a key scientific activity often neglected in the social sciences). Since methods of analysis are continuously being improved, archive data also allow the application of new or improved analytic methods to existing data sets. For example, Whelan and Whelan (1984) applied new methods for the analysis of social mobility to existing data already analysed by an earlier researcher. A third advantage of archive data is the possibility they open up for carrying out comparative research across space or time.

Possible contents of an Irish social science data archive

The potential contents of quite a rich data archive exist in Ireland. Among the obvious data sources and series are the following.

Central Statistics Office

The potential contributions of the CSO include the EOLAS and SAPS databases as well as primary data sets such as those emanating from the Household Budget Survey, the Labour Force Survey and other surveys. It would also be valuable to include a 0.1 per cent or 1 per cent sample of the census material in an archive.

Teagasc

The annual Farm Management Survey which provides both technical and social information on a representative sample of Irish farms could be included in a national data archive.

The Economic and Social Research Institute

The ESRI Survey Unit has accumulated over 200 surveys on a wide variety of topics since it was set up in 1966. Most of these are ad hoc inquiries related to particular projects but some are ongoing such as the School Leavers' Survey (annual since 1980), the EU Consumer Survey (monthly since October 1995), the ESRI/IBEC Monthly Business Survey and the bi-annual Investment Survey (since 1976). Resources have never permitted the creation of an externally accessible data bank to hold and document these data. Copies of certain files have occasionally been made available to researchers when resources allowed.

Universities

Staff at several of the universities have collected important data sets on a variety of topics. For example, the Social Science Research

Centre at University College Dublin collaborates with the ESRI to conduct the Irish versions of the International Social Survey Programme studies. This internationally co-ordinated programme of research involves the conduct of surveys on various agreed themes or modules and the international database is created and co-ordinated by the University of Köln. To date, modules have been conducted on work; inequality; the role of women; the environment; the role of government; religion and national identity.

Administrative data

Various government departments and agencies collect and publish statistics which could usefully be available from a national data archive. These include the Department of Social Welfare (numbers of participants on schemes, expenditure, unemployment); the Revenue Commissioners (distribution of taxation and income levels); the Department of Health (operation of the health services; mortality and morbidity data); and the Department of Education (examination statistics, numbers in education).

Why has an archive not emerged in Ireland?

Given the advantages to social science of an archive and the existence of much of the basic material required, it is reasonable to ask why a national social science data archive has not been set up in Ireland. The following factors seem to me to be relevant.

First, the number of social science researchers in Ireland has been and remains quite small. The archiving business enjoys considerable economies of scale in setting up facilities and training staff. If the number of depositors and users is small, then cost per user or per data set will be high.

Second, agencies involved in data collection are concerned about the implications for privacy and confidentiality of the existence of an archive. One spectacular breach of confidentiality could have disastrous long-run consequences for a body engaged in data collection on an ongoing basis. Data collection agencies are particularly concerned about breaches of confidentiality in respect of data on firms. Given the small size of the Irish economy, it would be very difficult to anonymise data on firms sufficiently to protect their identity without seriously impairing the value of the data for research purposes.

Third, the time and trouble imposed on the researcher who collected the original data can be considerable. The information must be tidied, organised and fully documented. All the 'special features' such as unusual missing values which all data sets acquire in the course of the first analysis must be recalled and written down. These tasks can represent a substantial burden for which there is little recompense at present either financially or in the form of academic prestige. It has been suggested that the deposit of a data set at an archive should be counted as a sort of publication and recognised for promotion and other purposes.

Fourth, the actual resource costs are not negligible. An archive needs a core of experienced staff, equipment etc. For example, the Data Archive at the University of Essex had a budget of £370,000 and a staff of twenty-five in 1992. While an Irish operation could be smaller, there is still a minimum size below which it would not be possible to go.

Fifth, the way social science research is funded in Ireland militates against 'public goods' such as an archive. Almost all research is funded by policy agencies to guide their management decisions. They have little direct interest in making the data they have funded available to all comers. Indeed, they may have genuine concerns about the manner in which the data could be used by opposing groups. What if the data are inappropriately used? Does the originator of the data acquire a long-term responsibility for checking and policing their use?

How can we make progress?

Given these obstacles, how can we make progress towards the establishment of an Irish social science data archive? To some extent, we benefit from being latecomers to this activity. Compared with earlier times it is today much easier to handle and document the data. Hardware procedures have become easier and more universal (e.g. compression software such as PKZIP for diskettes, writable CD-ROMs). Software has also become more portable and user-friendly (e.g. SPSS portable files).

This means that it will be somewhat easier to set up an archive. However, it does need an ongoing commitment of resources: all previous attempts based on goodwill have come to nothing. I reckon that a minimum scale would require three staff plus a base and equipment – say £100,000 per annum. Contacts with Essex or other European archives would be very beneficial in setting up procedures and systems. The recently inaugurated Large Scale Facilities Programme of the EU should be helpful in arranging and funding these contacts.

The first step would be to conduct a survey of potentially available data sets in Ireland. Then, one should start by archiving the most demanded data and make sure new data sets are added as they are collected. Finally, one could work back to include data of historical interest as time permits.

The clear benefits of an archive to social science research in Ireland would make this a very worthwhile initiative. Every effort should be made to secure support and funding for it.

References

Whelan, C. T. and B. J. Whelan (1984), *Social Mobility in the Republic of Ireland: A Comparative Perspective*, General Research Series Paper No. 116, The Economic and Social Research Institute, Dublin

Economic and Social Statistics for Twentieth-Century Ireland: An Integrated Database

MARTIN W. DOWLING AND LIAM KENNEDY

Introduction

Writings on history and the social sciences in Ireland have enjoyed a remarkable expansion during the last three decades. Within this broad literature, quantitative studies have assumed increasing importance. An implication of these wholly desirable developments has been that individual researchers have compiled customised data sets, independently of each other, at some cost and with little potential for reuse in further research. Recognising both the problems of duplication of effort and the opportunity for economising on resources, a group of historians at Queen's University of Belfast conceived the idea of a database of Irish historical statistics. The child of this thinking is the massive database of social and economic statistics on Ireland which is described below.

Background

The history of the project, in outline form, is as follows. From an initial suggestion by Max Goldstrom regarding the desirability of a large historical database, the concept of an integrated database of nineteenth-century statistics (1821–1911), with an advisory panel of leading scholars from Ireland and Britain, was designed by Liam Kennedy, as were the two successful applications for resources for the project to the Economic and Social Research Council. The first grant was received in October 1990 and the second in 1993, with the latter allowing coverage of the database to be extended from 1911 through to 1971 (thereafter many statistical sources are in machine-readable form). While the ESRC was the main source of funds – direct grants from that body amounted

to a quarter of a million pounds over a period of five years –
Queen's University also aided the project through the provision of
equipment (a work station and a scanner) and staff assistance. The
project got formally under way in October 1990 when Margaret
Crawford was appointed the first research officer for a term of
three years. Her brief included selection of the computer software
to be used and design of the database management system. For a
variety of reasons, including the availability of specialist expertise
within the university computing centre, INGRES was the choice
of software. Subsequent research officers have included Martin
Dowling and Paul Ell. The project was overseen by a management
group consisting of K. D. Brown, L. A. Clarkson (elected chair-
person), Max Goldstrom (business manager), Liam Kennedy and
later Margaret Crawford. On the initiative of Max Goldstrom, a
number of publications were projected, the most important of
which is a volume of essays on the Great Famine. This draws
directly on the rich regional and subregional materials contained
in the database.

Aim of the project

While the project had a number of subsidiary objectives, the
essential ambition was to produce an integrated database of Irish
historical statistics that would be a research resource for the wider
academic community. The justification for such a facility, which
could be accessed via the Data Archive at the University of Essex,
hinges on economies of scale. In principle it makes sense to create
a comprehensive database of economic and social statistics which
can be used, and reused, by current and future generations of
scholars, rather than individuals being obliged to construct their
individual data sets *ab initio*.

Users

In practice of course the extent to which a public resource of this
kind is used by scholars depends crucially on the relevance of its
contents to the user's needs and its user-friendliness. A prior condition is that potential users become aware of the existence of this

resource, which is one of the reasons for writing this paper. The contents, design and methodology of the twentieth-century database are described in detail below, which allows potential users to form their own judgements. But there is no doubt that the economic and social variables encompassed by the database are of a kind likely to be of relevance to a wide range of scholarly inquiries. These include demographic information, agricultural statistics, trade and production data and crime statistics.

Components of the database

The database comprises the following components:

- a user's guide describing the database and giving an overview of its development and structure. (This paper is based largely on the text of the user's guide.)
- a code book, which gives the coding scheme for the spatial units in the database. This is available in WordPerfect 6.0 for DOS format.
- five documentation volumes, which describe the series of tables in the database, the sources used in each table, and the notes and alterations associated with those sources. These are available as document files in WordPerfect 6.0 for DOS format.
- diskettes containing the tab-delimited ASCII data files referred to in the documentation volumes.
- graphics image files of prefaces and introductions in the sources which give important background information and in some cases analysis of the data contained in the database. These are available in *.gif format.

The database at a glance

The data is divided into the following five categories: Census of Population data, Registrar General's data, Agricultural Statistics data, Census of Industrial Production data, and Trade Statistics data. The database is composed of tables holding data from each of the five sources. These tables are briefly described as follows:

I. Census Material (county and county district spatial units at decade intervals)

POPULATION_TOTALS
Population by sex in each county district.

HOUSING_TOTALS
Housing by status and value of buildings in each county district.

RELIGION, RELIGION_AGE
Religion by age and sex of the population of each county district.

BIRTHPLACE_CD, BIRTHPLACE_COU, BIRTHPLACE_NI
The county of birth and county of residence of the population.

IRISH_LANGUAGE
Speakers of the Irish language in each county district

AGE
The age structure of the population of each county district.

CONJUGAL
The conjugal status of the population of each county district.

FAMILYAGE1_IR, FAMILYAGE2_IR, FAMILYCOU_IR, FAMILYREL1_IR, FAMILYREL2_IR
The classification of families by duration of marriage, age and religion of spouses, and children born in each county.

DEPENDENCY_IR
The number of dependent children in families in each county.

OCCUPATIONCOU_IR, OCCUPATIONCOU_NI
Occupational classification of the population of each county.

INDUSTRYOCCCOU_IR, INDUSTRYOCCCOU_NI
Industrial classification of the occupations of the population of each county.

II. Registrar General Materials (county data at yearly intervals)

VITAL STATISTICS
The numbers of births, deaths and marriages by sex in each county.

DEATH_AGE
The age of death by sex in each county.

DEATH_CAUSE
The cause of death by sex in each county.

INFANTMORT_1, INFANTMORT_2
Infant mortality in each county.

MARRIAGE_AGE
The age of marriage of brides and grooms in each county.

III. Agricultural Statistics (county and county district data for discontinuous sets of yearly intervals)

CROP_CD, CROP_COU, CROPSIZE_1, CROPSIZE_2
The various types of crops on various farm sizes in each county district or county.

STOCK_CD1, STOCK_CD2, STOCK_CD3, STOCK_COU1, STOCK_COU2, STOCK_COU3, STOCK_COU4, STOCK_COU5, STOCK_SIZE1, STOCK_SIZE2, STOCK_SIZE3, STOCK_SIZE4
The various types of stock on various farm sizes in each county district or county of the Republic of Ireland and in Northern Ireland as a whole.

FARMLABOUR_1, FARMLABOUR_2A, FARMLABOUR_2B, FARMLABOUR_3, FARMLABOUR_4A, FARMLABOUR_4B, FARMLABOUR_4C
The various types of farm labour (family, non-family, permanent, temporary) by age and sex in each county of the Republic of Ireland and Northern Ireland as a whole.

FARMMACHINES_1, FARMMACHINES_2A,
FARMMACHINES_2B, FARMMACHINES_2C,
FARMMACHINES_2D, FARMMACHINES_2E,
FARMMACHINES_3A, FARMMACHINES_3B,
FARMMACHINES_3C, FARMMACHINES_3D
The numbers of various types of farm machinery employed on
farms in each county of the Republic of Ireland and Northern
Ireland as a whole.

IV. Census Industrial Production Material (national data at yearly
intervals)

OUTPUT_IR, OUTPUT1_NI, OUTPUT2_NI, OUTPUT3_NI
General tables showing gross and net output, costs of inputs includ-
ing wages and salaries by industry in the Republic of Ireland and
Northern Ireland.

CAPITAL1_IR, CAPITAL2_IR, CAPITAL3_IR, CAPITAL1_NI,
CAPITAL2_NI
Working fixed capital in each industry in the Republic of Ireland at
year end. Fixed capital increases and decreases in each industry.

FIRMSIZE_IR, FIRMSIZE_NI
Size of firms in each industry.

FIRMSCOU1_NI, FIRMSCOU2_NI, FIRMSCOU_IR
Number of firms in each county in each industry.

WAGES1_IR, WAGES2_IR, WAGES3_IR, WAGES4_IR,
WAGES5_IR, WAGES6_IR
Persons employed in each industry in the Republic of Ireland dis-
tinguished by wages paid. Average earnings hours worked per week
in each industry in the Republic of Ireland.

V. Trade Statistics (national data at yearly intervals)

TRADECOM_1, TRADECOM_2, TRADECOM_3, TRADECOM_4,
TRADECOM_5, TRADECOM_6, TRADECOM_7, TRADECOM_8

The value of imports, exports and re-exports of various categories of each commodity to and from the Republic of Ireland and Northern Ireland.

TRADECOU_1, TRADECOU_2, TRADECOU_3, TRADECOU_4, TRADECOU_5, TRADECOU_6, TRADECOU_7
The total value of imports, exports and re-exports between the Republic of Ireland and Northern Ireland and various countries.

Design of the database

The remit of the project was to construct a relational database housed in a Database Management System (DBMS) called INGRES. The database will be held in this form at Queen's University of Belfast and at the University of Essex Data Archive. The INGRES software holds the data in a series of tables that are related to each other by a common field of geographical units. The DBMS allows data to be retrieved either through a 'Query by Forms' command menu or via SQL query language. The query language is designed for sophisticated manipulation and retrieval of data, and cannot be fully exploited without the necessary expertise. Nevertheless, users interested in simple retrieval of small data sets for use in a spreadsheet or other analytical software should have little difficulty mastering the necessary vocabulary. For those engaged in explorations involving the use of large amounts of data, the investment of time and effort may well be worthwhile. Moreover, as the project is an evolving one, further work is in progress on developing a more user-friendly front-end application.

However, it is not necessary to be familiar with the DBMS to make use of the twentieth-century database. The database exists in two forms: as a series of INGRES tables and as a collection of source-specific ASCII files. The tables in the database have been constructed from bibliographically tagged tab-delimited ASCII files. Users of the data may consult the documentation and acquire only those data from the bibliographic source tables that interest them. Both are clearly presented in the documentation volumes.

The tables in the database have been structured according to four constraints:

1. The database must be geographically relational, so that all
    tables must contain a column with spatial unit codes. In
    some cases this required significant manipulation of the
    original source.

2. The database must dovetail in content and form with the
    nineteenth-century database of Irish historical statistics cur-
    rently being completed in the Department of Economic
    and Social History at Queen's University of Belfast.

3. The database must be consistent in structure through time
    for given types of data, so that meaningful temporal com-
    parisons are possible for the user.

4. The database must be as comprehensive as possible, anti-
    cipating the needs of as wide a research community as
    possible given time and resource constraints.

The requirement to create a relational database housed in the
INGRES DBMS has both advantages and disadvantages. The relational database software and SQL query language are powerful
tools for the selection of data from particular geographic units,
particular years, a specific range of values, etc. However, the database is not structured for immediate statistical analysis in spreadsheet or other statistical software, and some manipulation of the
data will be required of the statistically minded user once the data
is downloaded from INGRES.

Tension between the latter two constraints is also evident in the
contents of some tables. While in a well-designed database, each
table contains information that is related to a single item of interest, the source material itself is often more densely organised. In
addition, variations in source material over time mean that some
database tables are not as comprehensive as the original source in
certain years.

Methodology of data capture, verification and transformation

The transformation of printed source material into electronic
form proceeds in the following steps:

1. The tables selected are scanned. The project's heavy investment in scanning hardware and optical character recognition software introduced a bias in the selection of data. Data that was easily scanned and transformed into ASCII format was given a higher priority than data that was not systematically presented in printed sources or for which the physical reproduction of the original source was not clear enough for the software. Some small groups of data that were not scannable were manually typed.

2. The image files created by the scanner are then processed with optical character recognition software. Once the software has adapted to the particular font of the original source, this process proceeds more quickly. The process is slower if the original source is not clear or in poor condition. The end product of this process is an ASCII text file composed of the numbers and text scanned in the original source.

3. The numbers in these files are then verified to ensure against errors in the scanning and recognition process. The ASCII files are loaded into spreadsheet software and column and/or row totals in the files are compared with those given in the original source. The error rate is quite low. Occasionally this process uncovers errors implicit in the original source. In twentieth-century printed material computational errors are extremely rare.

4. The text in these files is then edited and checked for accuracy or replaced by pre-established codes. All geographically oriented text is replaced by code. In addition, codes for the various industrial groups in the Census of Industrial Production data and the occupational groups in Census of Population data are inserted into the files.

5. After similar data from various sources (e.g., population tables from all the census years) have been processed and coded, their structures are homogenised so that they reside in one or a small number of database tables. This may involve the transposition of columns and rows, or the summation of rows where the description of variables is more

specific in some sources (e.g., if age or wage bands become wider, or the different types of cattle are more generally specified). In some cases, slightly differently defined data are placed in the same column and the difference is specified in the notes to the table.

6. The homogenised ASCII files are then given a final check for accuracy and inclusiveness, stripped of word processing code and prepared for copying into the INGRES database table. Once the data is held in database format, a number of simple verification procedures using SQL query language (counts, lists of distinct variables, sums, etc.) are employed as a final check.

Spatial units in the database

Where possible, data has been collected for spatial units smaller than the thirty-two counties. The data in the nineteenth-century database applies to counties, baronies or poor law unions. In the twentieth century, the data applies either to the county or the county district, both of which are historically and geographically related to the spatial units of the nineteenth-century database. In addition, the twentieth-century database includes data which has been recorded or published only at the national level. This includes the trade statistics of Northern Ireland and the Republic of Ireland, and the respective Censuses of Industrial Production. While this data cannot be spatially related to data in other tables in the database, it will hopefully be valuable for many academic users.

A wide range of data is given at the county or national level. However, the dominant spatial unit in the database is the county district (CD). The county districts were small enough to give detailed geographical coverage for a significant range of data. The CD is an amalgamation of district electoral divisions (DEDs). CDs also have the advantage of being directly related to the boundaries of poor law unions and towns, the dominant spatial units in the nineteenth-century database. CDs are located within counties but not within the seven county boroughs in Ireland.

County districts were established under the Local Government (Ireland) Act of 1898. The spatial units to which they refer were

Figure 1: Spatial organisation of the database

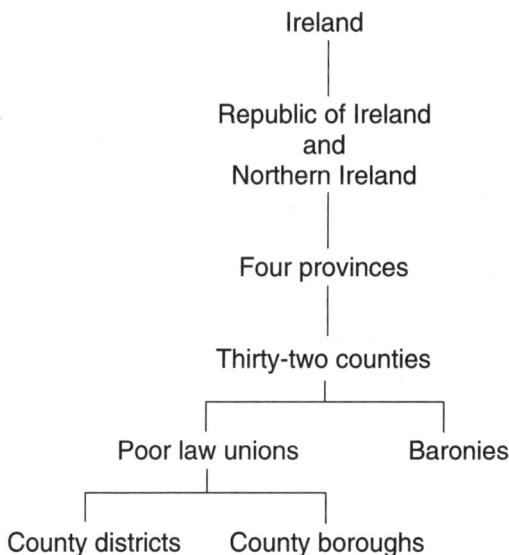

```
                        Ireland
                           |
                  Republic of Ireland
                          and
                  Northern Ireland
                           |
                   Four provinces
                           |
                 Thirty-two counties
               ┌───────────┴───────────┐
         Poor law unions            Baronies
        ┌────────┴────────┐
 County districts    County boroughs
```

originally sanitary districts established by the Public Health (Ireland) Act of 1878. The Public Health Act divided Ireland into urban sanitary districts and rural sanitary districts. Urban sanitary districts were created for the City of Dublin, all corporate towns and all towns with a population of 6,000 or more. The area of every poor law union, excepting those portions included in urban sanitary districts, formed rural sanitary districts. Under the Local Government Act sanitary districts were redesignated county districts, with the additional requirement that CDs be situated entirely in one county.

CDs were therefore created out of DEDs all of which are in the same county and the same poor law union. In all cases where poor law unions span counties or county boroughs, the county boundaries within the poor law unions were used to create the CDs. CDs are divided into rural and urban districts. While the former were created from the DEDs, the latter were created from the wards of the towns, the urban equivalent of the DED. Urbanisation and rural depopulation have resulted in the creation of many new urban CDs and the amalgamation of adjacent rural CDs in the twentieth century. By virtue of the Municipal Corporations Act of 1940, a number of urban CDs in Northern Ireland have been redesignated municipal boroughs.

Coding of data

In a relational database, it is necessary to make the selection of variables through a query language such SQL as simple and efficient as possible. To this end the counties, county boroughs and county districts have been coded. The coding scheme follows closely that devised by Margaret Crawford for the poor law unions in the nineteenth-century database; this will facilitate users interested in long-term change occurring in particular areas.

Aside from the geographical units, a number of other variables have been coded to allow for the more efficient retrieval of information. For example, a coding scheme is used for birthplaces outside Northern Ireland in the table BIRTHPLACE_NI. Coding schemes were also devised for the general occupational categories used in the tables OCCUPATIONCOU_IR, OCCUPATIONCOU_NI, INDUSTRYOCCCOU_IR and INDUSTRYOCCCOU_NI. And the trades and industries listed in the tables of the Censuses of Industrial Production were also coded.

Documentation

A database is only as good as its supporting documentation. For each table in the DBMS, the following information is given in the documentation volumes:

- a description of the columns of data giving their titles and a brief description of the data residing in those columns. The column titles are those used in the INGRES installations of the database in the Department of Economic and Social History and at the Data Archive in Essex. The titles are highly abbreviated and a short description of each heading is given.
- a bibliography of the source tables included in the INGRES table and the name of the ASCII text file which holds the data from each source table. These ASCII files allow users

interested in particular source material direct access to that material without the use of the relational database and its query language. The ASCII files are also the building blocks of the relational database.

* a description or quotation of footnotes, headnotes or other material in the original source pertaining to the INGRES table.

* an account of the alterations performed on the original source tables to align them with the structure devised for the INGRES table. The general rule for the construction of the database has been to restrict data selection to certain geographical units (see above) and to exclude subtotals, totals and percentages which can easily be re-created within spreadsheet software. Columns or rows in the source tables which have not been included in the INGRES table are noted.

Graphics image files

Each of the documentation volumes also includes a list of graphics image files of the tables of contents, prefaces and other notes relevant to the source tables in the original printed material. With both the individual documentation files and the graphic images, all relevant background material given in the original sources are available to the user. The graphics image files are scanned pages of the original source which cannot be accessed through word processing software. It is necessary to view these files with graphics image software such as LView Pro.

Conclusion

As is well known, there are advantages and disadvantages to the use of databases. For twentieth-century Ireland, where data is both rich and reliable, many inquiries employ a quantitative methodology. The database described here has considerable potential in relation to the needs of historians and social scientists engaged in longitudinal studies. It should be of particular value to those interested in making North–South comparisons, as the scope of the database extends to the whole island. Assembling data is both time consuming and expensive. Tapping into a major database for even part of one's data requirements could represent very substantial economies. To realise that potential means overcoming not only some minor technical barriers but also a cultural practice in the academic community which places undue emphasis on the researcher generating his or her own data. Increasingly that may come to be seen as an archaic value in the world of the Internet and large, generic databases.

Making Survey Data Accessible: A Report on a Project to Collate Irish Opinion Poll Data in a Machine-Readable Database

MICHAEL MARSH

The data collected by opinion poll companies is a unique and irreplaceable record of public attitudes and perceptions at a time of rapid change in Irish society. This material has not been collected for posterity, and the companies who carried out the surveys and for whom they were done will not themselves preserve the results in perpetuity. Already, some of it can be difficult to track down. Many old survey reports are stored in warehouses and some have already been lost. It is important to provide a permanent record of what currently exists, and to provide a means for integrating new material into this collection. These reports do not contain the original individual-level data. However, they do contain a wealth of analysis, typically comprising tables showing the breakdowns of responses according to social and political subgroups.

A number of studies have made use of questions asked repeatedly. For instance, Laver (1986) examined social patterns of party support, Borooah and Borooah (1990) assessed government popularity and Harrison and Marsh (1994) considered the popularity of party leaders. The data series used in such studies will be required for future researchers. At present, they have to be reconstructed anew from the original primary sources, or obtained from those who have already used them (in what may be an idiosyncratic form). There are also other series gradually building – for instance on divorce, or various items relating to social issues or Northern Ireland – which are time consuming to unearth. A single, well-constructed database will provide a significant incentive for further research in the area.

Research activity must be cumulative. A clear record of past activity can only be to the benefit of future efforts. A comprehensive collection of questions and answers provides a valuable resource for further survey research. A well-indexed collection will show survey researchers what has been done and will enable them to assess the possible impact of different question wordings in a particular area (see e.g. Marsh, 1992).

The yearbook of the Political Studies Association of Ireland, *Irish Political Studies*, has since its foundation reprinted opinion poll responses, at first for a limited set of questions asked in Market Research Bureau of Ireland (MRBI)/*Irish Times* polls and since 1994 for a comprehensive set of items from Irish Marketing Surveys Ltd (IMS)/Independent Newspapers Ltd and MRBI/*Irish Times* opinion polls. A recent survey of readers of *Irish Political Studies* carried out by the Political Studies Association of Ireland established the value of its data section – a substantial proportion of which is the opinion poll coverage – with 57 per cent of respondents describing it as 'very useful' and a further 31 per cent as 'fairly useful' (see *PSAI Bulletin*, No. 21, May 1995). This demonstrates that there is substantial academic interest in such materials.

The project described here has been funded by the Irish Social Science Research Council. It involves the collection and collation of reports of surveys of Irish public opinion since IMS started such polling in 1974, thus taking the series now published in *Irish Political Studies* as far back as possible. It seeks to collect all surveys done by IMS, MRBI and Lansdowne Market Research Ltd for newspapers (and, where possible, for private clients).

There is a need for such a collection to be as comprehensive as possible. Whilst some questions are asked regularly and others are asked only once, both types of material are important. The more ephemeral questions will be of obvious importance to future historians looking at particular events but even questions on particular events can be used to establish movements in popular attitudes on broader questions, such as trust in government and liberalism.

There is also a need to make the data accessible. The great advantage of a computerised database is that it makes it possible to find quickly a particular survey, and even more importantly, to trace questions on a particular topic. A database has been constructed, using the Macintosh program Hypercard which allows for both easy data entry and a user-friendly search and retrieve facility. This is described below.

Figure 1 shows the screen the user is faced with on opening the database. It provides a number of buttons, and clicking on any of these moves the user to any one of several different types of 'cards'. These are:

- survey cards, which provide information on individual surveys
- question cards, which provide information on individual questions within each survey
- a list of questions card, where the user can search the question database using keywords
- a list of surveys card, showing all surveys included in the database
- a button to initiate the process of entering data for an additional survey.

Figure 1 Entry card

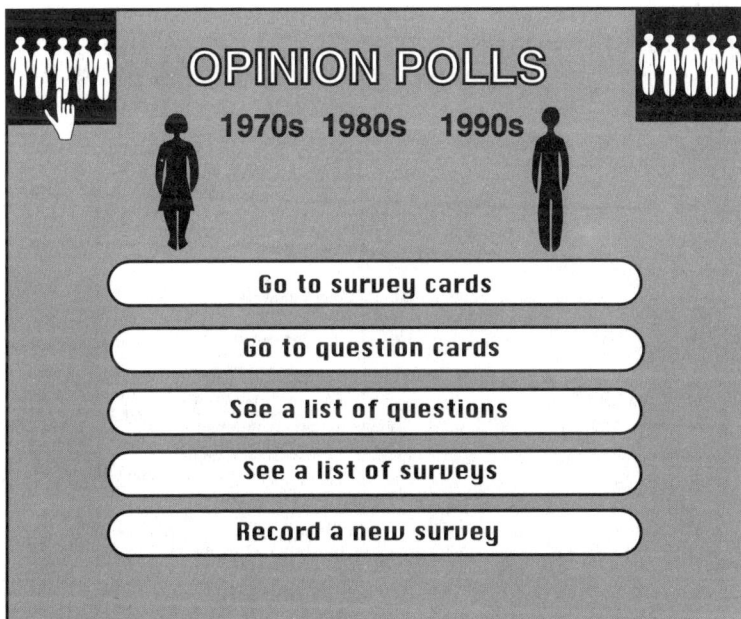

Survey information card

This is shown in Figure 2. It contains a number of fields in which particulars of a survey have been entered. These include the name of the company which carried out the survey, the code number (if any) of the survey, the client for whom the survey was done, the

Figure 2 Survey information card

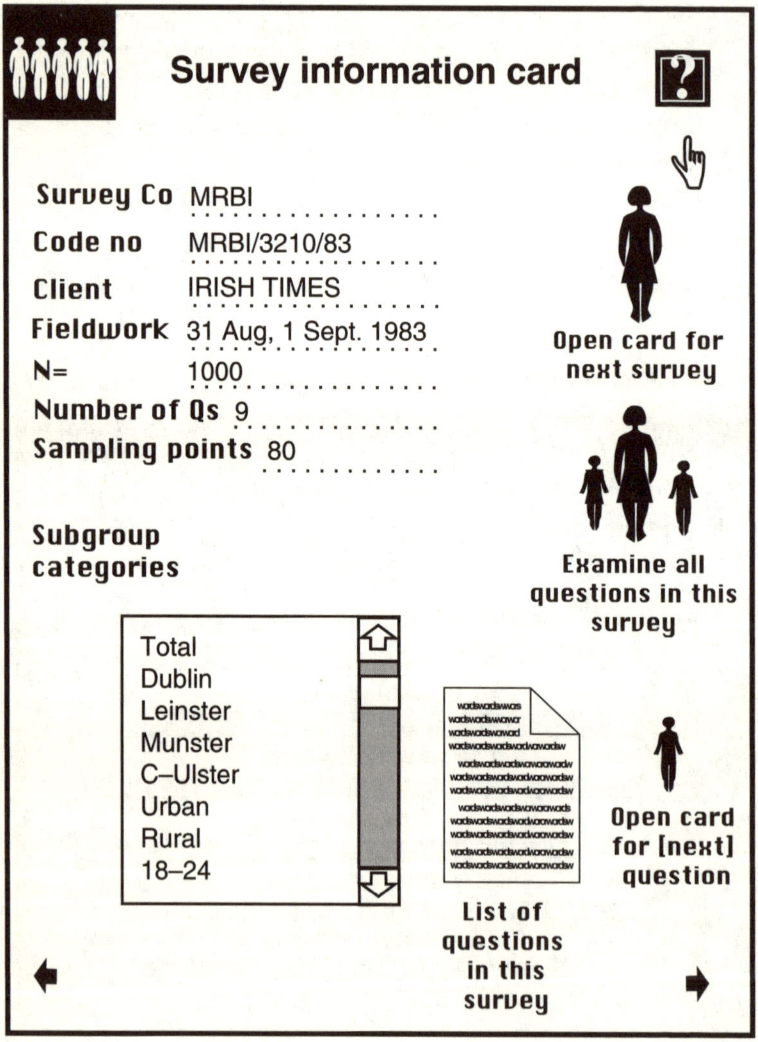

dates of fieldwork, the number of interviews, the number of questions asked, the number of sampling points, and the sub-groups of the population for which results are reported – men, women, farmers etc. The card also contains a number of buttons. One lists all questions asked in the survey; essentially it provides the full questionnaire (see Figure 3). Another displays all the question cards for the survey. Two more provide for the creation of new survey or question cards when new data is being entered.

Figure 3 Questionnaire display

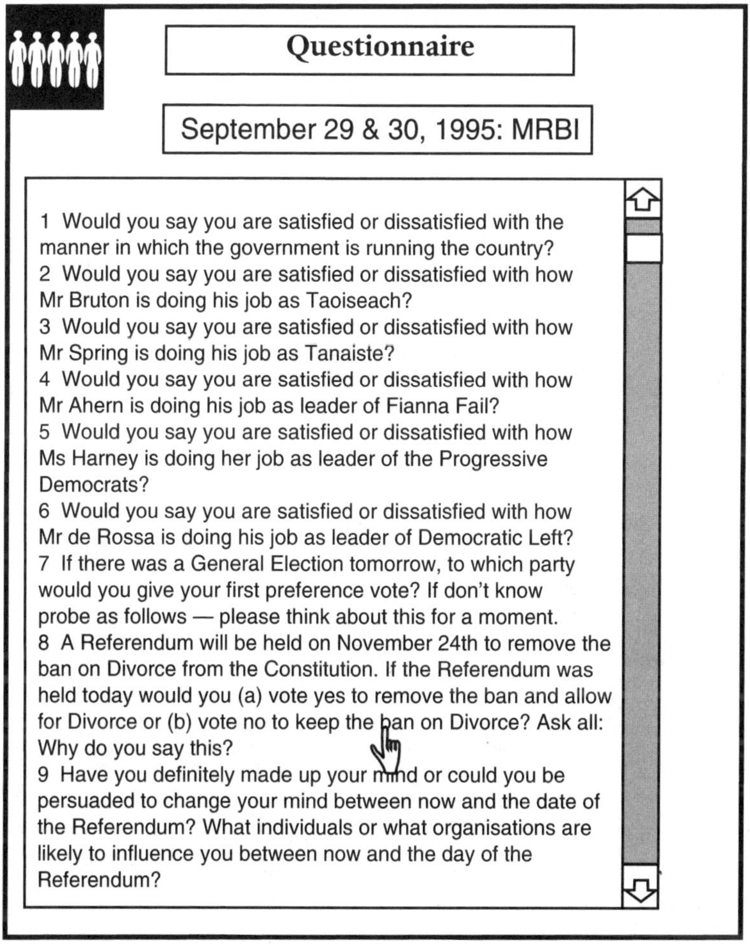

```
            ┌─────────────────────────────────────┐
            │           Questionnaire             │
            └─────────────────────────────────────┘

            ┌─────────────────────────────────────┐
            │    September 29 & 30, 1995: MRBI     │
            └─────────────────────────────────────┘
```

1 Would you say you are satisfied or dissatisfied with the manner in which the government is running the country?
2 Would you say you are satisfied or dissatisfied with how Mr Bruton is doing his job as Taoiseach?
3 Would you say you are satisfied or dissatisfied with how Mr Spring is doing his job as Tanaiste?
4 Would you say you are satisfied or dissatisfied with how Mr Ahern is doing his job as leader of Fianna Fail?
5 Would you say you are satisfied or dissatisfied with how Ms Harney is doing her job as leader of the Progressive Democrats?
6 Would you say you are satisfied or dissatisfied with how Mr de Rossa is doing his job as leader of Democratic Left?
7 If there was a General Election tomorrow, to which party would you give your first preference vote? If don't know probe as follows — please think about this for a moment.
8 A Referendum will be held on November 24th to remove the ban on Divorce from the Constitution. If the Referendum was held today would you (a) vote yes to remove the ban and allow for Divorce or (b) vote no to keep the ban on Divorce? Ask all: Why do you say this?
9 Have you definitely made up your mind or could you be persuaded to change your mind between now and the date of the Referendum? What individuals or what organisations are likely to influence you between now and the day of the Referendum?

All cards also contain a Home button in the top left-hand corner which returns the user to the opening card (Figure 1) and a Help button in the top right-hand corner.

Question card

This is shown in Figure 4. Each card contains a number of fields containing information on each question asked. These are: the question number (within the particular survey), the full wording of the question, the full set of answers provided, and the number of cases within each subgroup and percentages giving each option. For

Figure 4 Question card

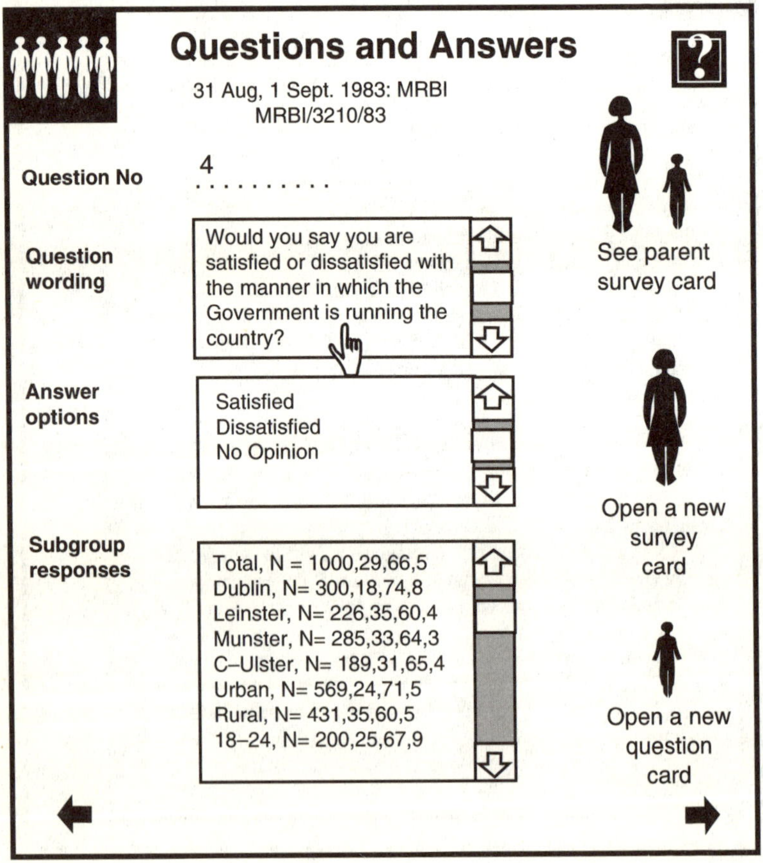

instance, in Dublin there are 300 respondents, and of these 18 per cent are satisfied, 74 per cent dissatisfied and 8 per cent don't know. This last field contains automatic checks that percentages add up to 100 (or at least fall within the 99–101 range), so that a check can be made against the original report. There is also an automatic check that a number is entered for each answer option. The card also shows the date and code number of the survey. There are also several buttons. These allow for the opening of new survey or question cards, or for the display of the survey card describing the survey to which a particular question belongs. Again, there are Home and Help buttons.

List of questions card

This is shown in Figure 5. The major scrolling field displays results from searches of the question database. The 'Find a question' button throws up a series of options which allow users to indicate what keywords they want to use in a search and whether the search is to take in the whole database or simply a particular year. The scrolling field displays some of the results from a search of the 1995 data using the keyword 'divorce' and shows questions, general marginals, date of each survey and company. The contents of this field can be printed using the 'Print field below' button. The 'List full results' button displays the contents of the subgroup analysis field from the selected question cards. The 'Excel table' button creates a tab-delimited file containing the breakdowns on each answer by the subgroups contained on the question card. This is displayed within the scrolling field but also saved to a separate file. The format is modelled on that employed in the data section of *Irish Political Studies*. This can be opened and manipulated by a spreadsheet program like Excel. Again, there are Home and Help buttons.

Survey listing card

Finally, as shown in Figure 6, there is a survey listing card, which simply displays all surveys contained in the database, first by code number, and then by company and dates of fieldwork. Buttons allow for searching and sorting.

Figure 5   List of questions card

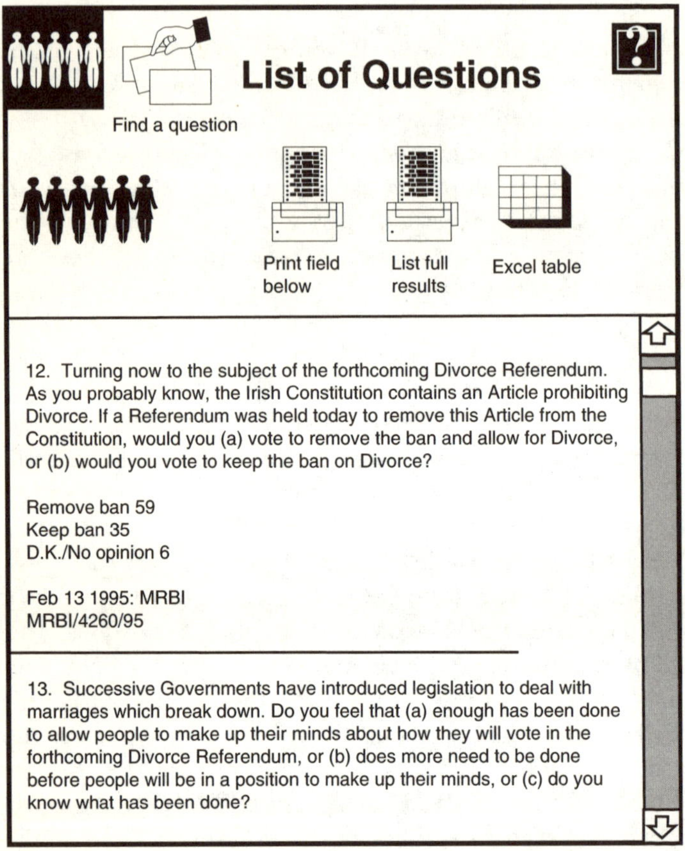

To date over sixty of the ninety or so MRBI national polls since 1977 and over one hundred of the IMS polls since 1974 have been entered into the database and work is continuing on tracing and including the remainder. There are plans to publish results from question series of most widespread interest (for instance, those on vote intention, leaders' popularity, attitudes to items on the 'liberal agenda' and Northern Ireland) and also to make the database itself available on disk, and eventually via the Internet.

Figure 6 Survey listing card

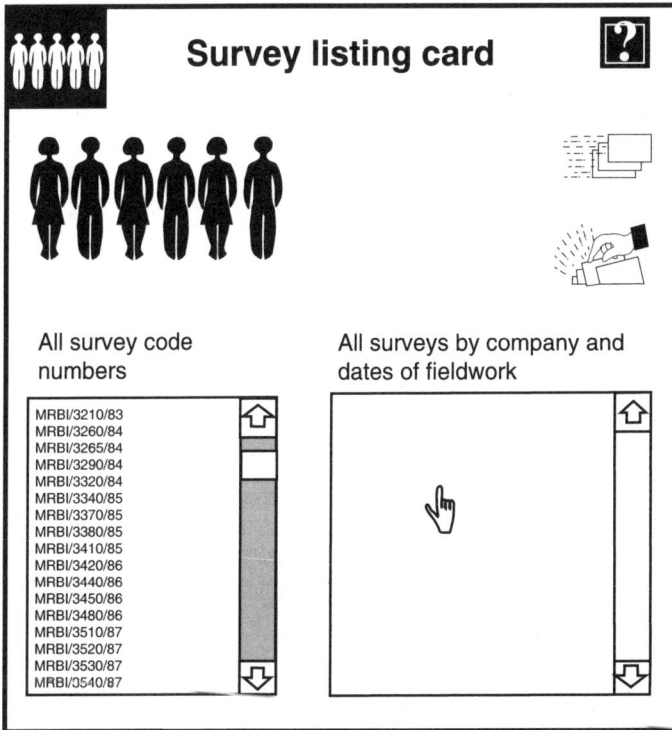

References

Borooah, V. K. and V. Borooah (1990), 'Economic Performance and Political Popularity in the Republic of Ireland', *Public Choice*, LXVII, pp. 65–79

Harrison, M. J. and M. Marsh (1994), 'What Can He Do For Us? The Popularity of Leaders and their Parties in Ireland', *Electoral Studies*, 13, 4, pp. 289–312

Laver, M. (1986), 'Ireland: Politics with Some Social Bases – An Interpretation Based on Survey Data', *Economic and Social Review*, XVII, pp. 193–213

Marsh, M. (1992), *Irish Public Opinion on Neutrality and the European Community*, Institute of European Affairs, Dublin, Occasional Paper No. 1

Access to European Data

DENISE LIEVESLEY

Introduction

This paper focuses upon the need for improved access to cross-national data for European research, and discusses the barriers which currently exist in obtaining access to such data. A number of European initiatives are taking place to try to improve data availability and these will be identified.

Recent years have seen a major increase in the demand for cross-national data to facilitate research on a European base. This is stimulated by an increasing 'internationalism' of research but it has been given a particular focus by the availability of European funding for cross-national studies through the European Union, the European Science Foundation and other funding bodies. A report on the social sciences in the context of the European Communities identified as a major barrier to an effective mobilisation of European social science 'the current gap between the quality of most national data and what is available at a European level' (European Science Foundation, 1991). It concluded that 'at a national level Europe is data rich' but that locating and accessing comparable data across different countries was both time consuming and subject to disappointment.

Obtaining data

Obtaining data on Europe is a complex task because of the wide variety in both the content and availability of official data.

Maffini (1990) suggested that five factors influence the distribution of official data: political, legal, administrative, economic and moral. Of these the administrative or organisational aspects of the government statistical system have a major impact on the availability of socio-economic data.

Government statistical systems can range from the highly centralised (such as Canada or New Zealand) through to the decentralised (such as the USA). Examples of both centralised and decentralised systems occur in Europe. In the centralised systems one agency is largely responsible for the collection and dissemination of official statistics whereas in the decentralised systems the responsibility is shared amongst a number of substantive agencies.

Statistical systems also vary in the extent to which they are regionalised. In some countries all of the data collection activities are carried out by one national agency (as in the Netherlands or Denmark) or by several national agencies (as in the UK) whereas in other countries these responsibilities are devolved to regional or local offices (as in Germany).

Understanding the organisation of statistics in a particular country presents problems since history and pragmatic decisions have often played their part. As an illustration the complex structure of the UK statistical system is outlined.

Two central departments – the Central Statistical Office and the Office of Population Censuses and Surveys (as from 1 April 1996 merged into the Office for National Statistics) – have major statistical responsibilities but alongside these about thirty ministries collect, collate, analyse and publish their own data. Additionally some twenty or so organisations such as the Bank of England and government departments in Scotland and Northern Ireland operate statistical offices. With the exception of the five Scottish government departments, twelve Northern Irish departments and the Welsh Office, there are no regional offices. However, somewhat confusingly because of the political decision to relocate central government, not all the 'central' statistical offices are based in London.

Unfortunately it is necessary to have a reasonable understanding of a country's statistical system in order to locate and obtain relevant data. The more centralised systems have the advantages that it is usually easier to discover what data are available, data will probably be collected using consistent methodologies and data will be disseminated from one central point. On the other hand decentralised and regionalised systems may provide more detailed and relevant data for local areas.

Content

Socio-economic data are derived typically from four sources: censuses, surveys, registers and administrative sources. However the
composition of the package of data and the relative importance of
the different methods vary considerably both across countries and
within countries according to different fields.

If we examine the availability of data on income and expenditure, for example, we find that in the UK these data are collected
via a continuous Family Expenditure Survey, in the Netherlands a
periodic survey is conducted whereas in Sweden income data
are available from population registers. None of the European
Union countries collect income data in their censuses, in contrast
to the USA.

Take population data as a second example: several European
countries no longer hold a census but rely on register data and
large-scale surveys to provide information on the structure and
mobility of the population. The Netherlands, for example, last
held a population census in 1971. In Denmark a census is held
which is entirely computer based using data on both individuals
and dwellings derived from seven sources (central population
register, the central register of buildings and dwellings, the central
register of enterprises and establishments, the register of wages
and salaries, the register of income, the register of employment
and the register of educational results) which are linked through
personal identity numbers.

Despite a major initiative on the part of the European Union to
try to harmonise census taking in member countries, conventional
censuses were taken in only nine countries and two of these
(France and Italy) departed from the attempt to synchronise the
dates. In Germany a micro census was taken of 1 per cent of the
population.

The content of the census data collection has been influenced
to some degree using the United Nations recommendations but
major differences still occur within the European Union. In particular, substantial differences occur in the provision of data on
housing facilities, economic characteristics of individuals and geographic indicators (Langevin et al., 1992). Practice differs widely

across Europe with respect to the conduct of census coverage checks and other validation studies. Thus the availability of information with which to adjust census data is very variable and not surprisingly the extent to which adjustments take place, being influenced by internal political factors within countries, also differs greatly.

Although initiatives of the European Union through its Statistical Office, Eurostat, have resulted in greater co-ordination of member countries' statistical outputs, substantial differences still exist. The focus has been to harmonise the definitions and classifications being used but to date there have been relatively few attempts to standardise methodology. Thus the 'same' data collection exercise, such as the Labour Force Survey which is a requirement of membership of the EU, is carried out by face-to-face interviews in some countries and by telephone in others. The rules regarding the admissibility of proxy data also differ across countries. Such decisions do of course affect the response rates and other aspects of data quality.

The European Statistical Office seems to be strengthening its efforts to develop a Community statistical system in the framework programme for priority actions in the field of statistical information 1993–1997 (CEC, 1992a). The following aims are identified:

1. to implement a system of standards, methods and organisational structures which is capable of producing comparable, reliable and relevant statistics throughout the Community

2. to provide the European institutions and the governments of the member states with the information they need to implement, monitor and evaluate Community policies

3. to disseminate statistical information to Europe in general, to businesses and to all concerned with economic and social matters, to assist them in their decisions

4. to seek to improve the statistical systems in the member states and to support the development of statistics in the developing countries and countries which are changing over to market economies.

The European Union has pledged to 'take account of international statistical recommendations in the fields covered' so hopefully the initiatives should promote international comparability.

In some countries all, or most, of the data collection activities are carried out under legislation which makes participation compulsory. This is the situation in Canada and New Zealand. In other countries only some data collection exercises (commonly the census and economic statistical inquiries) are compulsory. As well as affecting the quality of the information collected this can also have an impact on the decisions regarding its dissemination. In general information provided under compulsion is distributed less freely than data provided voluntarily though obviously the particular wording of the legislation will be critical (in Canada, for example, there is a policy of providing public-use tapes from the census and surveys whereas in New Zealand legislation prevents the dissemination of unit record data outside government). We will return later to a discussion of this issue in relation to Europe. An important factor in the decision whether to make individual-level data available will be the exact wording of the undertaking regarding confidentiality which is given to respondents. In fact this varies for different surveys both *within* and *between* European countries.

Geographic information systems require data disaggregated to small units or preferably geo-referenced. Obviously this need cannot easily be met if data are collected using surveys whereas administrative sources or censuses provide more scope for disaggregation if statistical confidentiality concerns can be satisfied.

A major barrier to the linking of different data at a local or regional level is the use of areal definitions which do not match on the various data sources. This problem is particularly likely to occur in countries with decentralised systems. In the UK, for example, although there is a supposedly 'standard' definition of the regions which is used as the basis of many government statistics, other departments have found the definition to be not well suited to their administrative needs. Departments, therefore, use a variety of regional maps which primarily reflect the structure of the service in question. In particular, the Department of Health uses regional health authorities which do not correspond to standard regions and the Department of Employment uses yet a third system.

Availability

' Users' expectations are often shaped by their experiences of obtaining data in other countries, particularly the USA where the culture is one of open government. Data sharing is encouraged because of an overriding acceptance of data being a public good. In Europe the situation is much more complex, with a complicated web of relevant legislation on data access (relating to confidentiality, data protection and copyright) interacting with different cultural values. In Europe the norm is for data not to be made available unless a convincing case can be made otherwise. For an example of the sort of case which is required, see Marsh et al. (1991) which argues that the risk of disclosure from the UK census of population can be reduced to an acceptably low level. The government has accepted this argument and two samples of anonymised records from the 1991 UK census are available as a consequence.

Different European countries, even those within the European Union, operate under very different legislation and this can dictate the extent to which data are made available. In several countries unit record data are not routinely distributed outside government departments. Taking the Labour Force Survey as an example, although it is carried out in all EU countries only three countries deposit the data in an archive for secondary analysis. There are, however, moves to try to locate data from all the Labour Force Surveys in Luxembourg in a database called the Luxembourg Employment Survey which would provide restricted access for registered researchers. This model has already been adopted in relation to income surveys.

Some countries, such as Finland and the Netherlands, have arrangements whereby academic researchers can be made temporary members of the staff of a government department in order to obtain privileged access to unit record data. Although these schemes are undoubtedly worthwhile they extend access to only a limited number of researchers.

As I have indicated, access to data, particularly to disaggregated or unit record data, is largely determined by the legislation operating in a country. In Austria, for example, a strict data protection law guarantees the right of individuals to confidentiality with respect to personal data. This means that some data – racial origin, political opinion, health, criminal record, sex life and religion – are especially protected and can be processed only if the legal system guarantees suitable protection. It also means that individual data gathered in surveys cannot be passed to anyone except staff directly involved in the collecting and processing of the data.

In contrast, the relatively new legislation in Germany (1987 Federal Act on Statistics) includes a statement that microdata can be made available to institutions for scientific research provided a number of conditions are met, notably that the data can only be identified with effort and investment in manpower, time and other costs that are unreasonably high.

De Guchteneire and Mochmann (1990) presented a compilation of reports from ten countries on data protection and data access which illustrate the diversity of contexts within which social researchers have to operate. More recently Eurostat has sponsored two international seminars on the topic of statistical confidentiality. The seminars ranged over ethical, legislative, administrative, technical and statistical aspects of the protection of anonymity. The proceedings have been published by Eurostat.

Again the picture is one of great diversity in the practice of making data available. A topic in the first seminar concerned the rights which Eurostat has in making data available which it has obtained under 'transmission legislation'.

There are initiatives to harmonise European Union law on data confidentiality and access. Some of these cut across the current practice of individual countries. In some cases the policies are beneficial to those who argue for freer access. For example a 1990 European Council directive requires official agencies in member states to make environmental data available at reasonable cost (CEC, 1990). According to Robert Worcester (1993):

> In these regulations 'information' includes 'anything contained in any records . . . '. It provides that the Department and all other Ministers of the Crown, government departments, local authorities and other persons carrying out functions of public administration, etc., and any public body

with public responsibilities for the environment, 'should make that information available to every person who so requests it . . . ' 'as soon as possible . . . ' and is responded to no more than two months after it is made . . . 'and if refused, specifies the reason for that refusal in writing'.

On the other hand a Council directive on the protection of individuals with respect to the processing of personal data and on the free movement of such data has been adopted (CEC, 1992b). The aim is to protect the rights of individuals especially their right to privacy. There are, however, concerns since the directive states that data can only be used for specified, explicit and legitimate purposes and not further processed in a way incompatible with those purposes. Of course, personal data protection is important but where possible research should be accommodated without incurring risks to individual respondents.

The situation with regard to data access is not static. Changes in legislation can have a major impact on what is made available as do changes in the pledges made to respondents relating to confidentiality. Public opinion on the right balance between the society's right to knowledge and the individual's right to privacy can also shift (as seen in the rise in concern in Sweden following alleged breaches of confidentiality). The prevailing ethos in a society can be crucial in determining what level of confidential information will be released.

There is a tendency within both Europe and the USA to attribute falling response rates to an increased public concern about confidentiality. There is, however, little concrete evidence that this is the main reason for the public's non-participation.

Another important factor is the attitude of the officials, the 'guardians' of the data. Fortunately, the principle that decisions about data should be formed not just by the current concerns of government but also by the needs of an informed society is gaining acceptance.

Encouraging statements about the importance of sharing data with external users and involving them in their agencies' work are being made by senior official statisticians across the world. Janet Norwood, then the US Commissioner for Labour Statistics, stated

in her American Statistical Association presidential address in 1989:
'Those who produce data must . . . maintain a dialogue with users.
This interaction enhances the effective use of data to understand
emerging trends and enables statistical agencies to keep their data
series relevant'. Similarly, the Director of Statistics in Sweden, Sten
Johansson (1990), wrote: 'Statistics bureaus also need an intimate
relationship with science both for improvement of statistical methods in various policy areas and to provide official statistics as an
infrastructure for social and related sciences'.

In a speech to the Confederation of British Industry on 19 May
1992, the Chancellor of the Exchequer discussed this issue:

> There is no conflict between efficient and well-funded pub-
> lic services and a thriving private sector. On the contrary we
> have always recognised that there are some services that only
> the public sector can provide. One such service is, of course,
> the provision of official economic statistics. There is no
> doubt in my mind that weaknesses and gaps in Britain's
> statistics have made the task of economic management more
> difficult. While we must always be careful to avoid adding to
> the burdens on business, it is vital that the Government
> should have the information it needs. But official statistics are
> produced not just for the Government, but for the benefit of
> business and for the public at large.

The United Nations Economic Commission for Europe adopted
'fundamental principles' during its 47th session in Geneva in 1992,
which included the following resolution:

> Official statistics provide an indispensable element in the
> information system of a democratic society, serving the gov-
> ernment, the economy and the public with data about the
> economic, demographic, social and environmental situation.
> To this end, official statistics that meet the test of practical
> utility are to be compiled and made available on an impartial
> basis by official statistical agencies to honour citizens' enti-
> tlement to public information.

Despite these admirable sentiments the ethos of providing information and sharing data is not universally accepted and countermanding pressures create uneasy tensions for data access.

Much government-collected information is increasingly being considered a commodity, in part because departments and agencies are operating with inadequate resources to conduct their work in the depth and quality they deem desirable and as a consequence are required to generate revenue. Sales of information are an obvious way of raising income.

Inge Feldback of Danmarks Statistik has stated (1992): 'The aim has been to become more businesslike and to produce statistics more to the demand of paying customers . . . Price policy becomes more important, copyrights more restricted and the number of privileged users tend to decline'.

David Rhind (1991) was pessimistic about these developments: 'The ownership of data seems inevitably destined to become part of the competitive process and, as such, to affect the abilities of those in education in particular to carry out research and teaching relevant to the needs of the outside world except by the forging of intimate and individual links with data suppliers'.

It is essential that charging policies for data are discussed with, and understood by, users. There are particular difficulties in setting charges in monopolistic situations because of the problem of determining 'value for money'. Harlan Onsrud (1992) discusses these difficulties: 'After a government department has gained an exclusive right to provide a specific service which generates income, there is little incentive for the government bureaucracy to improve that service. If a monopolistic government service makes a net income for the government, the operation is almost certain to be inefficient'. Onsrud goes on to argue that cost recovery arrangements create bureaucratic overhead and legal disincentives to the sharing of information. Trewin (1991), though positive about most changes, discusses some of the difficulties of what he calls the 'marketing culture' from the perspective of an official statistician.

Obviously, there is a major conceptual and financial difference between charging to cover the marginal costs of data dissemination and charging in order to offset some of the costs of data collection. Decisions such as these must take account of the fact that different users have very different resources at their disposal and that a reasonable charge for some users may prove to be totally unafford-able for others. Research which is in the public interest could be reduced as a result.

Other threats to data access exist. In some countries transmission of data outside of the country is not permitted without the explicit permission of a registrar. This might be deemed 'data sov-ereignty'. The other side of the coin is 'data imperialism' whereby commercial organisations from wealthy countries purchase the rights to data from developing or transitional countries thus deny-ing others access to the data.

European initiatives

A number of initiatives have taken place within Europe either with the intention, or with at least the consequence, of improving access to data.

The European Science Foundation has established a number of scientific networks bringing together researchers from across Europe to conduct comparative research. Two such networks – one on Geographic Information Systems and the other on Beliefs in Government – have had a particular focus upon data availability and have discussed ways in which better comparative research could be fostered through improved access to high-quality harmonised and integrated data sets.

The same topic has been a theme of the discussions of the Standing Committee on the social sciences of the European Science Foundation which have also involved the National Science Foundation of the USA.

These debates were one of the reasons for the Universities of Durham and Essex (through the auspices of the National On-Line Manpower Information Service and the Data Archive respectively) submitting an application to the Economic and Social Research Council to establish a Resource Centre for Access to Data on Europe. The Centre was awarded funding and was established in January 1995 with five years' seed money from the ESRC. Its role is to enable researchers to identify data of interest to them and to try to assist them in accessing such data by acquiring the data and build-ing them into an integrated on-line database.

The Council of European Social Science Data Archives (CESSDA) is very conscious of the various threats to data access and is trying to counter them to promote the widest use of data internationally. The general principle of developing data capabilities and archives within countries rather than removing data is accepted. A data exchange agreement has been adopted to ensure that when possible data are available to researchers in other countries. Initiatives have been taken to develop an on-line integrated catalogue for data archives thus enabling researchers to browse a catalogue which would contain metadata on all of the individual archives' holdings. As might be anticipated language is a barrier to this since several of the European archives do not have catalogues in English, but funding has been obtained from the European Union and some progress is under way on the technical aspects of this work.

Individual archives are active in negotiating for low-cost access to data and promoting the use of data through high-quality documentation, educational activities etc. Unfortunately, data archives do not currently exist even in all Western European countries and as a consequence the situation is far from uniform. CESSDA has been active in trying to get new archives established.

A number of agencies both European (such as Eurostat and the UN Economic Commission for Europe) and international (including the International Labour Office, OECD and various UN bodies) have embarked upon programmes to harmonise statistical outputs. These have had mixed results but there are a few remarkable developments, such as Intrastat (the new European system for compiling trade statistics) and Prodcom (the new European system to collect and publish the sales values classified by a standardised frame of products).

Other European initiatives include the establishment of two large-scale facilities in the social sciences at the Universities of Essex and Cologne. The beneficiaries of these centres will be researchers from across Europe who will be provided with access to the facilities, especially data, accompanying documentation and related unpublished papers, together with specialist published material, with a view to conducting comparative research.

The Eurodata Centre at Mannheim provides an excellent information service on sources of data which is very helpful to researchers who wish to embark upon research of a comparative nature.

Conclusion

Barriers to data access for cross-European research do exist for a variety of reasons, most notably those of confidentiality, copyright and commodification. Such barriers are more acute in relation to some countries' data than others. Similarly researchers in some countries have better facilities in order to aid them in the complex process of locating, identifying and obtaining relevant data. There are, however, a number of European initiatives which should help in removing some of the barriers to data access.

References

(This paper draws heavily on one by Lievesley and Masser, 'Geographic Information in Europe: An Overview', presented at Urban Regional Information Systems Association Conference, Atlanta, USA, July 1993.)

Commission of the European Communities (1990), *Council Directive on the freedom of access to information on the environment*, COM(90) 313, CEC, Brussels

Commission of the European Communities (1992a), *Programme for priority actions in the field of statistical information 1993–1997*, COM(92) 395 Final, CEC, Brussels

Commission of the European Communities (1992b), *A revised proposal for a Council Directive on the protection of individuals with regard to the processing of personal data and the free movement of such data*, COM(92) 422 Final, CEC, Brussels

Day, D. L. (1991), 'The Impact of Future Social and Technological Trends on the Dissemination of Census Bureau Information', *IASSIST Quarterly*, 15, 3/4

European Science Foundation/Economic and Social Research Council (1991), *The Social Sciences in the Context of the European Communities*, European Science Foundation, Strasbourg

Feldback, I. (1992), 'Dissemination and Marketing: Danish Developments', *Proceedings of 1992 Statistics Users Council Annual Conference*, Imac Research, Lancaster House, More Lane, Esher KT10 8AP, Surrey UK

de Guchteneire, P. and E. Mochmann (eds.) (1990), *Data Protection and Data Access*, North Holland, Amsterdam

Johansson, S. (1990), 'Information Needs for the Market and for Democracy', *Journal of Official Statistics*, 6, 1

Langevin, B., F. Begeot and D. Pearce (1992), 'Censuses in the European Community', *Population Trends*, 68, pp. 33–6

Lievesley, D. (ed.) (1993), *Proceedings of the International Seminar on Statistical Confidentiality*, Eurostat, Luxembourg

Maffini, G. (1990), 'The Role of Public Domain Databases in the Growth and Development of GIS', *Mapping Awareness and GIS in Europe*, 6, 1, pp. 49–54

Marsh, C., C. Skinner, S. Arber, B. Penhale, S. Openshaw, J. Hobcraft, D. Lievesley and N. Walford (1991), 'The Case for Samples of Anonymised Records from the 1991 Census', *Journal of the Royal Statistical Society (A)*, 154, 2, pp. 305–40

Norwood, J. (1989), 'Statistics and Public Policy: Reflections of a Changing World', ASA Presidential Address

Onsrud, H. J. (1992), 'In Support of Open Access for Publicly Held Geographic Information', *G.I.S. Law*, 1, 1, pp. 3–6

Rhind, D.W. (1991), 'The Next Generation of Geographical Information Systems and the context in which they will operate', unpublished paper delivered to the European Science Foundation Workshop on European Research in GIS, Davos, Switzerland

Trewin, D. (1991), 'Strategic Directions in Marketing in a Government Statistical Office', *Proceedings, International Statistical Institute Session, Cairo*, ISI, Voorburg, the Netherlands

Worcester, R. (1993), 'Data Management Policies for Global Environment Change', *ESRC Data Archive Bulletin 53*

Appendix 1

Speakers, chairpersons and participants

Speakers

Séamus Clince, Principal Officer, Centre for Management and Organisation Development, Department of Finance, Dublin

Mark Conrad, Archivist, Center for Electronic Records, National Archives and Records Administration, Washington DC

Martin W. Dowling, Research Fellow, Department of Economic and Social History, Queen's University Belfast

Eithne FitzGerald, TD, Minister of State at the Office of the Tánaiste

Anne Gilliland-Swetland, Assistant Professor, Department of Library and Information Science, University of California, Los Angeles

Ken Hannigan, Senior Archivist, National Archives of Ireland

Liam Kennedy, Reader in Economic and Social History, Queen's University Belfast

Denise Lievesley, Director, ESRC Data Archive, University of Essex

Michael Marsh, Senior Lecturer in Political Science, Trinity College Dublin

Donal Murphy, Director General, Central Statistics Office, Dublin

Matti Pulkkinen, Head of Data Section, National Archives of Finland

Brendan J. Whelan, Head of Survey Unit, Economic and Social Research Institute, Dublin

Chairpersons

David V. Craig, Director, National Archives of Ireland

John A. Jackson, Professor of Sociology, Trinity College Dublin and Chairman, Social Science Research Council, Royal Irish Academy

Dermot Keogh, Jean Monnet Professor of European History, University College Cork

Patrick A. McNutt, Professor of Political Economy, University of Ulster

Richard Sinnott, Director, Centre for European Economic and Public Affairs (CEEPA), University College Dublin

Participants

Ger Ahern, United Nations Training School

Sophie Carey, Department of Social Studies, Trinity College Dublin

Geoffrey Cook, Department of Social Policy and Social Work, University College Dublin

Marianne Cosgrave, National Archives

Angelique Day, Institute of Irish Studies, Queen's University Belfast

Ann de Valera, Irish Society for Archives

Breige Doherty, Derry City Council

Brian Donnelly, National Archives

Sr Magdalena Frisby, Mercy International Centre
Michael Gallagher, Department of Political Science, Trinity College, Dublin
Treasa Galvin, Department of Sociology, Trinity College Dublin
Myles Geiran, Institute of European Affairs
Rachel Granville, College Archives, University College Cork
Damien Hannan, Economic and Social Research Institute
Sue Hemmens, Christ Church Cathedral
Helen Hewson, Department of Geography, Trinity College Dublin
Sr Dominique Horgan, Dominican Generalate
Donal Igoe, Department of Political Science and Sociology, University College
    Galway
Ger Kenny, Department of Finance
Stuart Kinsella, Christ Church Cathedral
Lee Komito, Department of Library and Information Studies, University College
    Dublin
Victor Laing, Military Archives
Fr Leo Layden, Holy Ghost Fathers
Rena Lohan, National Archives
Sr Frances Lowe, National Library of Ireland
Mark McCarthy, Department of Geography, University College Cork
Naomi McCay, Centre for Social Research, Queen's University Belfast
Sheelagh McCormack, Mercer Library, Royal College of Surgeons in Ireland
Michael McGreil, Department of Social Studies, St Patrick's College, Maynooth
Karl Magee, National Archives
Jane Maxwell, Manuscripts Department, Trinity College Dublin
Sr Baptist Meany, Presentation Sisters
Della Murphy, National Archives
Máire Nic Giolla Phádraig, Department of Sociology, University College Dublin
Gregory O'Connor, National Archives
Matt O'Donovan, Irish Society for Archives
Colette O'Flaherty, National Library of Ireland
Betsy Omidvarn, National Bahá'í Centre
Siobhan O'Rafferty, Royal Irish Academy
Myra O'Regan, Statistics Department, Trinity College Dublin
An tÁth. Ciarán Ó Sabhaois, Mainistír Cnoc Iosaef, Ros Cré
Una O'Sullivan, Royal Commission on Historical Manuscripts, London
Jonathan Pratschke, Department of Sociology, Trinity College Dublin
Mary Prendergast, Institute of Public Administration
Tom Quinlan, National Archives
Carol Quinn, Boole Library, University College Cork
George Rowley, Department of Education
Eda Sagarra, Economic and Social Research Institute
Jerry Shea, Tree Council of Ireland
Virginia Teehan, College Archives, University College Cork
George Walker, Dublin Institute of Technology, Kevin Street
Monica Wallace, Department of Transport, Energy and Communications
Sean Ward, Office of the Comptroller and Auditor General

Appendix 2

Further sources of information available on-line

Listed below are a number of sites on the World Wide Web which contain further information on the issues discussed in this volume.

Government of Ireland   http://ireland.iol.ie/irlgov/

National Archives of Ireland   http://www.kst.dit.ie/nat-arch/

The Data Archive (University of Essex)   http://dawww.essex.ac.uk/

Center for Electronic Records (National Archives and Records Administration, USA)   http://www.nara.gov/nara/electronic/

EDINA (Edinburgh Data and Information Access, University of Edinburgh)   http://edina.ed.ac.uk/

IASSIST (International Association for Social Science Information Service and Technology)   http://datalib.library.ualberta.ca/iassist/

Social Science Data Archive, Australian National University (Excellent guide to worldwide social science resources available on-line)   http://ssda.anu.edu.au/

Social Science Information Gateway (University of Bristol)   http://sosig.esrc.bris.ac.uk/

Glossary*

American Standard Code for Information Interchange (ASCII) A coding scheme which specifies bit patterns for computer processible information. The ASCII standard uses 7 of the 8 bits a byte to define the codes for 128 characters.

appraisal The process of determining the value and thus the final disposition of records, making them either temporary or permanently preserved as archives (see *archives, records management*).

archives The non-current records of an organisation which have been appraised for permanent preservation because of their continuing evidential, legal or informational value. A place in which archival records are permanently maintained.

to archive The process of identifying, segregating and transferring old or inactive computer data from an active computer system onto off-line digital storage.

arrangement, archival The organisation of archives, records and manuscripts in accordance with accepted archival principles.

computer disk, read-only memory (CD-ROM) A compact laser disk with read-only memory, designed for recording document images and information for mass distribution.

data Symbols or representations of facts or ideas that can be communicated, interpreted or processed by manual or automated means. Often associated with electronic data or with statistics or measurements.

database A set of data, consisting of at least one file or a group of integrated files, usually stored in one location and made available to several users at the same time for various applications.

database management system A software system used to access and retrieve data stored in a database.

data file An organised collection of related data, usually arranged into logical records that are stored together and treated as a unit by a computer; *or* related numeric, textual or graphic information that is organised in a strictly prescribed form and format. Used in contrast to text documents that may be recorded on electronic media.

data processing Systematically performing a series of actions with data. May be done by manual, mechanical, electromechanical or electronic (primarily computer) means. Often used interchangeably with automatic data processing.

data protection Ensuring that personal information created and maintained in electronic format is used only for the purpose for which it was compiled and allowing the individual to inspect such personal information for the purposes of verification and amendment where necessary.

data set A group of related electronic records that are organised and treated as a unit. Also used interchangeably with data file.

---

* In compiling this glossary we have drawn on definitions previously used by Anne Gilliland-Swetland and the Center for Electronic Records, National Archives and Records Administration, Washington DC, in some cases adapting them to an Irish context.

disposal   The actions taken regarding temporary records after their retention period expires and consisting usually of destruction or occasionally of donation to an eligible person or organisation (see *disposition, records management*).

disposition   The actions taken regarding records no longer needed in current office space. These actions include transfer to temporary storage facilities pending appraisal or transfer for permanent preservation to an archives (see *appraisal, disposal, records management*).

electronic records   Records stored in a form that only a computer can process (see *records*).

electronic records system   Any information system that produces, processes or stores records by using a computer. Often called an automated information system.

e-mail (electronic mail)   The process or result of sending and receiving messages via telecommunications links between computer terminals.

Extended Binary Coded Decimal Interchange (EBCDIC)   A coding scheme which specifies bit patterns for computer-processible information for electronic records created on IBM mainframe and other large computers.

finding aid, archival   A cataloguing and retrieval system which lists and describes archival material in order to facilitate use.

freedom of information   A legal right of free access to information contained in the records documenting the activities of government agencies, and a legal obligation on the part of government agencies to provide this information on demand, subject to restrictions relating to personal privacy and state security.

Geographic Information System (GIS)   A system bringing together maps and data regarding natural, demographic and cultural resources in any number of layers to display data visually.

government records   The records created by the functioning of government agencies (see *records*).

Internet   An international 'network of networks' with search and downloading facilities (see *network*).

metadata   'Data about data', or composite documentation that exists about all electronic systems operating within an institution (see *data*).

network   A system linking two or more computers and other electronic devices through the use of electrical cabling or telecommunications links.

records   All information-bearing media, regardless of physical form or characteristics, made or received by an organisation in connection with its official functions and appropriate for preservation by that organisation or its legitimate successor as evidence of the organisation, functions, policies, decisions, procedures, operations or other activities of that organisation or because of the informational value of the data in them.

records management   The planning, controlling, directing, organising, training, promoting and other managerial activities related to the creation, maintenance, use and disposition of records to achieve adequate and proper documentation of the activities of the record-creating organisation (see *appraisal, archives, disposal, disposition*).

relational database   A database design that allows direct relationships between any two data elements.